Adaptations for
SAXON MATH
Course 2

Adaptation by
Pat Wrigley

Teaching Guide

For Use with *Saxon Math Course 2*

Appropriate for
- Self-contained and inclusion classrooms
- Special education
- Title 1 students
- At-risk students
- Resource classrooms
- Adult education

A Harcourt Achieve Imprint

www.SaxonPublishers.com
1-800-284-7019

ISBN 1-5914-1850-X

Printed in the United States of America

1 2 3 4 5 6 7 8 202 13 12 11 10 09 08 07 06

SAXON MATH™

From the Author

Forty years of teaching has led me to a few discoveries that are worth sharing. And as a recovering math-phobe for the past 18 years, I find I have become positively evangelical about communicating my joy at having discovered Saxon math.

My first twelve years in the classroom were spent teaching grades 4 through 8 in general education, both public and private schools. I was effective in teaching language arts, social studies, and foreign languages, and even reasonably good in science; but math was a problem. I later received my Master's Degree in Special Education of Physically Handicapped Students. Since then, most of my teaching experience has been as a resource specialist in the middle school or junior high setting.

Before I discovered Saxon, I had become very discouraged teaching math. My students could learn the material but couldn't retain it. Thus, I spent two years writing my own textbook, stressing mastery plus maintenance of skills learned. Then, at a math conference one summer, I discovered that Stephen Hake and John Saxon of Saxon Publishers had not only arrived before me, but had surpassed my finest efforts.

In the past 18 years of teaching with Saxon books, I have learned to love teaching math. Without hesitation I can say it is my favorite subject. Every teacher should get such satisfaction from his or her work! In unlocking the mysteries of math I get to give my students a running jump at self-esteem. My students know they are terrific and show it. I always was a competent teacher, but until I started using Saxon math, I never touched the lives of my students so effectively.

I have learned a great deal since my first year of using Saxon math, and you will too. If the individualized program I have developed overwhelms you at first, start with only what you can comfortably use. You will grow with it as I did. I hope this teaching guide is helpful. It will be a resource to refer to as you refine your approaches. And please share new approaches with me. I'm always fine-tuning my program.

Acknowledgements

I would like to recognize the people who saw value in my work and encouraged it from the beginning. They are Frank Wang and Deborah Hicks from Saxon Publishers, and my principal at Vallejo High, Phil Saroyan. Thanks too, to the editors at Harcourt Achieve who polished my raw material: Deborah Diver, Margot Hetrick, and Marc Connolly. Finally, a special thanks to my younger daughter Sarah, whose special needs inspired my work. Also thanks to my older daughter, Rebecca, who was an invaluable assistant in my writing.

Pat Wrigley
Retired Resource Specialist
Vallejo, California

SAXON MATH™

Table of Contents

The Saxon Philosophy. 1

Saxon Math Adaptations 2

Components of the Adaptation 3

   Saxon Math Course 2 Textbook 3

   Teaching Guide 3

   Student Reference Guide 3

   Lesson Worksheets. 4

   Tests 4

   Targeted Practice 4

   Answer Key 5

   Manipulatives and Reference Charts 5

   Supplementary Materials 5

   Annotated Lesson Worksheet 6

   Sequence Sheet 8

Preparing Your Classroom 9

Program Implementation 10

   A Self-Paced Approach 12

      the beginning of the class period .14

      the middle of the class period. 14

      the end of the class period 15

      "how to succeed" chart 16

      homework. 17

      testing 17

      recycling 18

      grading 19

      testing schedule 20

      sample recording form 21

An Inclusion Approach 22

    power up 22

    lesson worksheets 24

    new concept 24

    practice set 24

    written practice 25

    supplemental practice 25

    tests 25

    decreasing usage of support materials 26

Teaching English Language Learners 27

Classroom Management 28

    Classroom Aides 28

    Motivation 29

    Involving Parents 30

    Rules for Success 30

Teaching Strategies 31

Charts

    Targeted Practice 80

    Fraction Activities 82

    Concept Posters 83

Individualized Education Plans 84

    Short-term Learning Objectives 84

    Sample IEP form 87

Suggested Reading 88

Suggested Viewing 88

Related Organizations 89

The Saxon Philosophy

We believe that people learn by doing. Students learn mathematics not only by watching or listening to others, but by doing the problems themselves. In the Saxon program, mathematics is taught (and learned) just as a foreign language or musical instrument is taught—incrementally with continual practice.

Therefore, the three most important aspects of the program are incremental development, continual practice and review, and frequent, cumulative assessment. Incremental development refers to the division of topics into small easily understood pieces called *increments*. Major concepts are not taught in single lessons but are developed over time; thus, students are not expected to completely understand concepts the first time they are presented. Instead, new concepts are distributed throughout the year along with the previously learned concepts. Continual practice and review means that fundamental skills and concepts are practiced and reviewed throughout the year, helping ensure that students retain them. Assessments are given after every five lessons and are cumulative in content.

Many mathematical skills take time to develop, and students must be given the opportunity to develop and to master these skills with the practice provided in the problem sets. Each problem set contains only a few problems that practice the new increment, while the remaining problems, which increase in difficulty as the year progresses, provide practice of the concepts previously presented.

*The three most important aspects of the program are **incremental development, continual practice and review**, and **frequent, cumulative assessment**.*

Saxon Math Adaptations

Saxon Math Course 2 Adaptations provides support materials for the instruction and exercises in the *Saxon Math Course 2* program to assist struggling learners. The *Adaptations* materials are designed to ensure success for a range of students, including students who have difficulties with the following:

- visual-motor integration

- fine motor coordination

- spatial organization

- receptive language

- number transpositions in copy work

- getting started

- verbal explanations

- distractibility

- math anxiety

The *Adaptations* materials provide alternate teaching strategies, assistance for the lessons and tests, student reference materials, and extra practice on select topics. They can be used in a variety of classroom settings, including inclusion and pullout programs.

This guide explains how to take advantage of the *Adaptations* materials according to the needs of your classroom. It offers support for minimal to maximal implementation depending on the instructional model, teacher resources, students' abilities, and classroom materials.

Adaptations materials provide alternate teaching strategies, assistance for the lessons and tests, student reference materials, and extra practice.

Components of the Adaptation

The *Adaptations* materials described below are designed to support the *Saxon Math Course 2* program, and they must be used in conjunction with the Student Edition, Teacher's Manual, and Instructional Masters.

saxon math course 2 textbook

The textbook serves as the "backbone" of the program.

The textbook reinforces the basic mathematical concepts and skills that students learned in previous math courses. Concepts, procedures, and vocabulary that students will need in order to be successful in upper-level algebra and geometry courses are introduced and continually practiced. Daily mental math and problem-solving exercises enhance students' repertoire of skills and increase their mathematical power. *Adaptations* students use the Student Edition textbook every day.

teaching guide

*Use the Teaching Guide **in conjunction** with the Teacher's Manual.*

The Teaching Guide should be used in conjunction with the Teacher's Manual. This guide contains detailed information on how to implement the adaptation, as well as classroom management strategies, grading guidelines, and teaching strategies and hints. The guide is intended for teacher use only. *Please note that the Teaching Guide is not intended as a substitute for the Teacher's Manual; instead it explains how to modify the curriculum for struggling students.*

student reference guide

Daily use of the reference guide promotes memory of important math concepts.

Many students have difficulty memorizing facts such as weight equivalences and characteristics of geometric figures. To ease the burden of recalling information, the *Saxon Math Adaptations Student Reference Guide* includes charts, formulas, conversions, techniques, definitions, and other mathematical facts. As students grow familiar with the guide, they will gain confidence and become more proficient math students.

A four-page reference card is part of the mainstream Saxon Math program. The *Adaptations Student Reference Guide*, however, contains much more information; provide one for each struggling student.

lesson worksheets

Lesson worksheets, the "heart" of the adaptation, reduce the amount of work that students must transfer from textbook to paper.

Just as the written practice is the "heart" of the Saxon textbook, the lesson worksheets are the heart of the adaptation. They include teacher notes, a brief summary of the New Concept, and formatted workspace for both the Practice Set and the Written Practice. The lesson worksheets also provide clues to help students complete the problems. (See pages 6 and 7 for an annotated sample lesson worksheet.)

The lesson worksheets provide a consistent approach to concepts by the teacher, aide, substitute teacher, or parent. They reduce the amount of work that students must transfer from textbook to paper, reducing copying errors and the amount of time required to complete assignments. The lesson worksheets also contain more concise explanations, with simpler vocabulary than that used in the textbook. For some concepts, the lesson worksheets provide alternate problem-solving methods. **Students, however, must still refer to the textbook when completing the lesson worksheets.**

tests

Cumulative tests are administered on a regular basis. Each test has been adapted in a manner similar to the lessons—into a formatted worksheet. Unlike the lesson worksheets, test worksheets are stand-alone; that is, they contain the full text of problems as well as suggested strategies for working the problems. If students do not have enough workspace to complete the test problems, allow them to show work on an attached page. The answer should still be written in the answer box.

supplemental practice

Supplemental practice provides valuable practice of new concepts.

Struggling students benefit greatly from the additional practice of new concepts. This practice will not provide mastery, but it will make each concept more recognizable when it appears in subsequent lessons. Three different types of supplemental practice are provided:

- **Targeted Practice** worksheets provide additional practice of concepts that are typically more difficult to understand. Targeted Practice worksheets are laid out in a format similar to the lesson worksheets and may contain instruction or teacher notes. (See page 80 for a list of topics and lessons supported by Targeted Practices.)

- **Fraction Activities** employ manipulatives to help students reach a concrete level of understanding about fractions, decimals, and percents. (See page 82 for a list of topics supported by Fraction Activities.)

- **Quick Tests** are short quizzes which may be given at the beginning of the class period in place of Facts Practice. These tests familiarize students with the basic contents of the *Adaptations Student Reference Guide* and help seed their visual memories with necessary mathematical facts.

answer key

Because the lesson worksheets adapt the Student Edition textbook, the answers to all Practice Set and Written Practice problems are identical to the textbook answers. An answer key, however, has been provided for the Supplemental Practice worksheets.

manipulatives and concept posters

Manipulatives help teach difficult abstract concepts.

Concept Posters provide a quick, visual reminder of concepts learned.

Manipulatives are tools used to help teach difficult abstract concepts in concrete ways. The *Adaptations* Manipulative Kit is an optional purchase, but it is highly recommended since manipulatives are fully incorporated into the program. The Teaching Hints (beginning on page 31) and teacher notes on selected lesson worksheets explain the intended use of various manipulatives as well as identify the appropriate lessons in which to introduce them.

The Concept Posters are small posters that give facts and information that may be used in several ways: posted around the room for student reference, enlarged and used as posters, or copied for students to have individual copies close at hand. (See page 83 for a list of concept posters.)

supplementary materials

Several adaptations-specific pages are included:

- The **Sequence Sheet** shows all the assignments in correct order and helps self-paced students to advance through a course on their own. The first column on the sequence sheet lists the lesson worksheets; the second column lists the Targeted Practices and Fraction Activities; and the third column lists the tests. (See page 8.)

- A **Parent Letter** should be sent home at the beginning of the year describing the Saxon program, its requirements, and goals. Obtaining parental involvement is often crucial to students' success.

- **Recording Forms** are suited for the specialized grading scheme (see Grading on page 19).

- The **"How To Succeed" Chart** givens students a better understanding of how their daily work habits influence their success or failure in class.

- A **Graduation Certificate** is a reward for completion of a textbook.

- **Class Rules for Math** establish clear rules and expectations at the beginning of the school year to help ensure student success as well as reduce discipline problems. A handout such as this one could be discussed in class and then sent home to be signed by both students and parents.

- **Tips for parents, teachers, and students** will be useful during student/teacher conferences, parent/teacher conferences, and conferences between special population teachers and regular education teachers. These tips apply not only to math, but to all subject areas.

Annotated Worshet

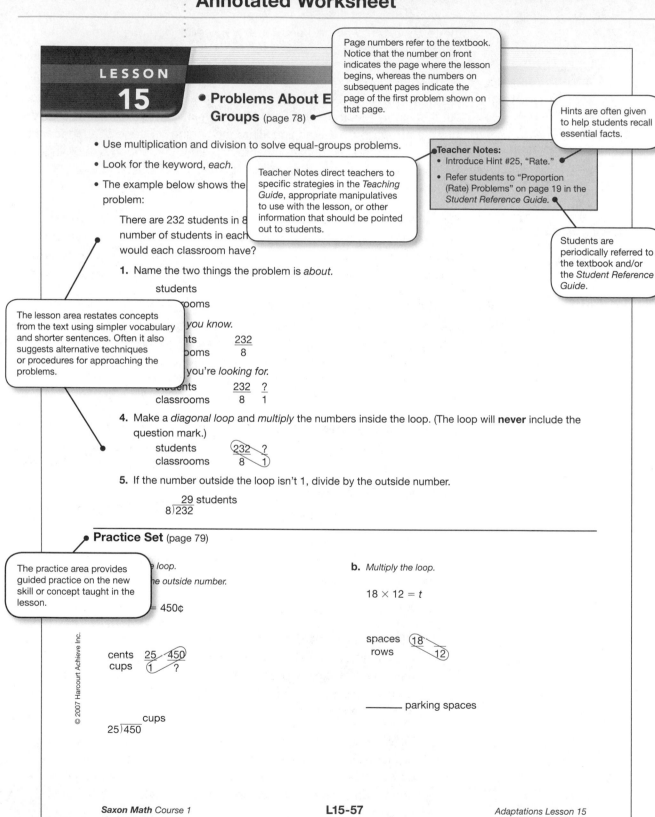

Page numbers refer to the textbook. Notice that the number on front indicates the page where the lesson begins, whereas the numbers on subsequent pages indicate the page of the first problem shown on that page.

Hints are often given to help students recall essential facts.

LESSON 15

Problems About E[qual]-Groups (page 78)

- Use multiplication and division to solve equal-groups problems.
- Look for the keyword, *each*.
- The example below shows the [...] problem:

Teacher Notes:
- Introduce Hint #25, "Rate."
- Refer students to "Proportion (Rate) Problems" on page 19 in the *Student Reference Guide*.

Teacher Notes direct teachers to specific strategies in the *Teaching Guide*, appropriate manipulatives to use with the lesson, or other information that should be pointed out to students.

Students are periodically referred to the textbook and/or the *Student Reference Guide*.

There are 232 students in 8 [...] number of students in each [...] would each classroom have?

1. Name the two things the problem is *about*.

    students

    [class]rooms

The lesson area restates concepts from the text using simpler vocabulary and shorter sentences. Often it also suggests alternative techniques or procedures for approaching the problems.

[...] *you know.*

    [stude]nts   232

    [class]rooms   8

[...] you're *looking for.*

    students   232 ?

    classrooms   8   1

4. Make a *diagonal loop* and *multiply* the numbers inside the loop. (The loop will **never** include the question mark.)

    students   232 ?

    classrooms   8   1

5. If the number outside the loop isn't 1, divide by the outside number.

$$8\overline{)232} \quad \frac{29}{}\text{ students}$$

Practice Set (page 79)

The practice area provides guided practice on the new skill or concept taught in the lesson.

[...] *loop.*

[...] *he outside number.*

[...] = 450¢

cents   25 450

cups   1 ?

$$25\overline{)450} \quad \underline{\quad}\text{cups}$$

b. *Multiply the loop.*

$$18 \times 12 = t$$

spaces   18

rows   12

_____ parking spaces

Saxon Math Course 1   **L15-57**   *Adaptations Lesson 15*

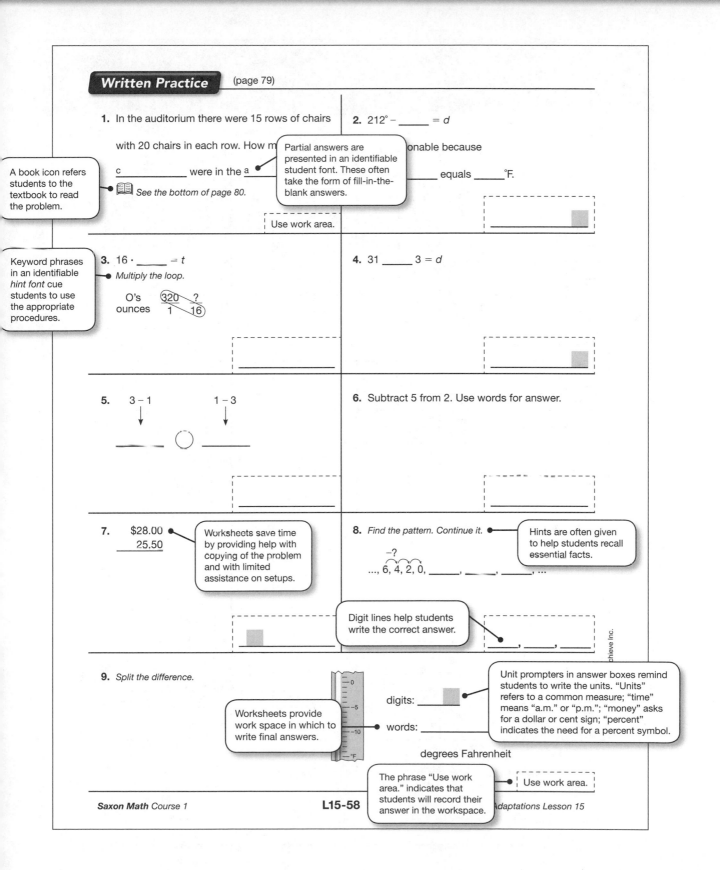

Written Practice (page 79)

A book icon refers students to the textbook to read the problem.

1. In the auditorium there were 15 rows of chairs with 20 chairs in each row. How m_____ onable because

c _____ were in the a _____

📖 See the bottom of page 80.

Use work area.

Partial answers are presented in an identifiable student font. These often take the form of fill-in-the-blank answers.

2. 212° − _____ = d

_____ equals _____°F.

Keyword phrases in an identifiable *hint font* cue students to use the appropriate procedures.

3. 16 · _____ = t

Multiply the loop.

```
O's        320      ?
ounces      1       16
```

4. 31 _____ 3 = d

5.   3 − 1   1 − 3

6. Subtract 5 from 2. Use words for answer.

7. $28.00
        25.50

Worksheets save time by providing help with copying of the problem and with limited assistance on setups.

8. *Find the pattern. Continue it.*

..., 6, 4, 2, 0, _____, _____, _____, ...

Hints are often given to help students recall essential facts.

Digit lines help students write the correct answer.

9. *Split the difference.*

Worksheets provide work space in which to write final answers.

digits: _____

words: _____

degrees Fahrenheit

Unit prompters in answer boxes remind students to write the units. "Units" refers to a common measure; "time" means "a.m." or "p.m."; "money" asks for a dollar or cent sign; "percent" indicates the need for a percent symbol.

The phrase "Use work area." indicates that students will record their answer in the workspace.

Use work area.

SEQUENCE SHEET

Lesson	Targeted Practice	Test	Lesson	Targeted Practice	Test	Lesson	Targeted Practice	Test	Lesson	Targeted Practice	Test
1	1(a, b, c)		31	31		61			91		
2	2		32			62			92		
3	3		33	33		63			93	93	
4			34			64	64		94		
5			35	35	5	65	65	11	95		17
6	6		36			66			96	96	
7			37	37		67			97	97	
8	A		38			68	68		98	98	
9	9		39			69	69		99	99	
10	10		40		6	70		12	100	100	18
Inv.1	B		Inv. 4			Inv. 7			Inv. 10		
11	C		41			71			101	101	
12			42			72			102	102	
13	13		43	43		73			103		
14	14		44			74			104		
15	15, D	1	45	45	7	75	75	13	105		19
16	E		46			76			106		
17	17		47			77			107	107	
18	19		48	48		78	78		108		
19			49	49		79			109	109	
20	20	2	50	50	8	80		14	110		20
Inv. 2			Inv. 5			Inv. 8	Inv. 8		Inv. 11		
21	21		51			81			111	111	
22	F		52	52		82	82		112		
23	23		53			83	83		113		
24			54			84	84		114		21
25		3	55		9	85	85	15	115	115	
26	26		56			86			116	116	
27	27		57	57		87	87		117		22
28			58			88			118		
29	29		59			89	89		119		
30	30	4	60	60	10	90		16	120		23
Inv. 3			Inv. 6			Inv. 9			Inv. 12		

Letters in Targeted Practice column refer to Fraction Activities.

Saxon Math Course 2   viii   *Adaptations Sequence Sheet*

Preparing Your Classroom

A well-organized, smoothly running classroom enhances instruction. Students should know where to turn in and pick up assignments, where to find manipulatives, and when it is appropriate to do these things.

Preparation tips:

- Use the **Adaptations** binder to organize the materials.
- Copy one week's worth of assignments at a time.
- Store manipulatives where easily accessible.
- Display reference charts on the days you teach related lessons.

Excepting this guide, the *Adaptations* Manipulatives Kit, and the *Adaptations Student Reference Guide*, the *Adaptations* program is an electronically-based program. The materials listed in the previous section are included on a single CD. For easier access, it is recommended that the optional *Adaptations* binder be purchased. This binder includes tabs for organizing the *Adaptations* materials. Prior to the start of the school year, the materials can be printed off the CD, three-hole punched, and inserted into the binder. This will greatly facilitate copying and organization throughout the year.

Each struggling math student should receive a copy of the *Adaptations Student Reference Guide* at the beginning of the year. If you copy each group of concepts onto a different color of paper (e.g., all the Geometry pages on yellow), students will have a visual reminder of where information appears in the reference guide. Students might also wish to keep a blank piece of paper with their reference guides to record additional definitions and formulas as needed.

The amount of support material you will need to copy depends on how many students are being supported and what kind of support you wish to give. Teachers may wish to copy a week's worth of lesson worksheets at a time for struggling students. If student usage fades throughout the year (see "Decreasing Usage of Support Materials" on page 26), the number of copies required each week will decrease. The lesson worksheets can be filed in hanging folders or three-hole punched and kept in a binder. Consider storing the lesson worksheets in an easily accessible location so that students can find them independently.

For many tactile and kinesthetic learners, use of manipulatives is indispensable. Consider establishing a station where students can access them with ease. The *Adaptations* Manipulative Kit can be purchased to supplement the program, or you can stock the station with any manipulatives you already have.

For visual learners, the Reference Charts can be enlarged for easier viewing. It is not necessary to post all the charts at the beginning of the year, but you might want to arrange the classroom so that there is a convenient place to post them at the opportune time. (See page 83 for a list of concept posters.)

Program Implementation

Like most of their peers, struggling students can learn math skills and applications; they simply have difficulty retaining what they have learned. Instructional modifications are necessary to help these students succeed. In a direct instruction setting, modifications are easy to implement and the results are dramatic. Most modifications can be accomplished successfully in an inclusion setting too. Some of the key modifications necessary to help students with special needs succeed in math are discussed below.

- **Simplify language.** To a struggling student, "flip the fraction" is more memorable than "give the reciprocal"; likewise "borrow" means more than "regroup." Always try to provide simple, clear language.

- **Maximize time focused on math; minimize time spent copying from the text.** The *Adaptations* lesson worksheets contain the problems students are required to solve. Not only does this save time for students, but it also helps reduce their frustration and the number of copying errors, number reversals, etc. Students may work directly on the lesson worksheets or attach another sheet of paper if more space is needed to solve a problem.

- **Provide and teach the use of reference material.** Reference material such as times tables and measurement facts should be readily available for classwork, homework, and tests. Students' visual memory will be enhanced, and gradually students will begin to rely less often on the reference material. More important, students will be able to do more difficult work by using this temporary "crutch."

- **Teach keywords as cues for word problems.** Struggling students often do not read well. If they can read digits and find keywords, however, they can solve most word problems. Teach students how to spot keyword vocabulary. For example, subtract for the words "profit," "difference," or "more than;" add for "together," "total," or "joined;" multiply for "product" or "double;" and divide for "per," "each," or "average." Post a keywords chart in the classroom to serve as a reminder.

- **Teach to a variety of learning modalities and skill levels.** Even within a special education setting, students vary in motivation, background, ability, and learning styles. Be sensitive to each student's individual needs. Whatever way a student learns best is the best way to teach him or her.

- **Build in a recycling option for concepts not mastered.**
  When students demonstrate that they have not mastered a skill, future concepts built on that skill will be in great jeopardy. It's much more productive to take the time to review concepts until they have been mastered than it is to continue in the hopes that students will eventually "get it."

- **Gear work towards students' "comfort zones."** This does not mean "easy" work, but work that is challenging yet not frustrating for each student. Behavior problems will diminish if students are able to do the work assigned. When students are not able to do their assigned work, their frustration will result in undesirable classroom behavior.

- **Teach shortcuts and strategies for approaching problems.**
  There are numerous ways to make computation less traumatic. Teach them. For example, in subtraction, borrowing across all zeros in one step is easy to learn and use. In column addition, find sets of ten. Use offset multiplication to simplify the work.

- **Task analyze complex concepts.** If students do not understand a concept, break it down into incremental steps. Students should not be expected to do this independently; this is the teacher's job.

- **Sharply limit lecture time to increase "learning by doing" time.**
  Keep "teaching time" brief. Give students just enough information to get them started. They will only learn by actually doing. You might feel better telling students everything you know about factors, but students won't. If students only need to list the factors of a number, don't tell them (at this point) about common factors or greatest common factors. Start them off and walk away. When students need more information, they will ask for it. Then they will be ready to listen because *they* asked for the help.

- **Incorporate manipulatives.** Use manipulatives as an efficient way to convey abstract concepts with a minimum of time and words. But be careful not to let manipulatives take over a lesson or you've lost the point. Consider the maturity of the student before choosing a manipulative. For example, gear-operated clocks are often used to teach elapsed time. Smaller clocks are less insulting to middle school students than large, primary-school clocks. Store manipulatives in the center of the room or another convenient location so that students will reach for them naturally.

Meeting the needs of struggling math students is challenging, but the *Adaptations* materials help teachers achieve that goal. *Adaptations* materials can be used effectively in individualized, self-paced learning environments or inclusive, mainstream settings. The outlines below give specific instruction for these two environments. These two implementations of the *Adaptations* materials can be used in whole or in part to tailor a program that best meets students' needs, based on students' abilities and availability of teacher aides and resources.

Teachers should read through both sections and choose the parts that will give the level of support required. In addition, some of the *Adaptations* materials may not be appropriate for enhancing all math students' understanding.

A Self-Paced Approach

Students using the lesson worksheets have demonstrated growth ranging from 18 months to 2-1/2 years per school year.

Normal academic growth for struggling students is six months or less per year, depending on the degree of disability. As a result, an ever-widening gap develops between students' academic level and actual grade level. Students who have been using the adapted worksheets in a self-paced "pullout" classroom have demonstrated growth ranging from eighteen months to two and one-half years per school year (as measured by the KETA or Woodcock-Johnson tests). It must be stressed, however, that results of this kind can only be achieved if students are required to complete daily homework assignments. After two years with the *Adaptations* program, many students are ready to move into regular mathematics courses.

With emphasis on positive reinforcement, this adaptation of the Saxon program promotes a calm, purposeful atmosphere with a high level of concentration and on-task behavior. Students take pride in their achievements and discipline problems are greatly reduced.

While individualized instruction should be the goal of special education, teachers who are unfamiliar with the program's content should begin the year with a "whole group" approach—all students working on the same lesson at the same time. This approach simplifies classroom management and allows the teacher to concentrate on teaching the content of a single lesson. Cooperative learning techniques may be used as well.

Begin the year with a "whole group" approach. Individualization will occur gradually as students progress at different rates.

Individualized instruction allows students to work at their own pace with the teacher facilitating and monitoring each student's progress. It may be achieved gradually, beginning with the first student who needs to "recycle" several lessons and falls behind the rest of the class. (Recycling is discussed on page 18.) The class will continue to subdivide as students progress at different rates. By this time the teacher will be familiar with the content of the material already covered by the fastest progressing students. Only the new lessons assigned to those students will be unfamiliar to the teacher.

An individualized approach requires:

- careful classroom management;
- familiarity with the program content;
- awareness of the needs of individual students; and
- the assistance of an aide to help with correcting papers and keeping records.

Individualization is beneficial because it:

- shifts the teacher's role from instructor to tutor;
- puts additional responsibility on students to manage tasks;
- allows students who are fast and accurate to move ahead;
- reduces frustration for students who need more time to master certain concepts;
- allows for the recycling that is necessary when content is not mastered; and
- makes gains of more than a year possible, narrowing the gap between functional level and target grade level.

Teachers should be available to give one-on-one instruction.

Teachers of individualized classes need to be free during the class period to give one-on-one instruction on new increments, to respond quickly to students asking for help, to discuss assignments with students, and to teach appropriate classroom behavior. An aide, teacher's assistant, or parent volunteer may be enlisted to check student work, to supply extra copies of lesson worksheets for recycling, to maintain portfolios of student work, and to do the record keeping. The aide may also watch for evidence of calculator use, repetition of certain errors, omission of lessons, etc.

the beginning of the class period

A daily short warm-up exercise helps occupy students while teachers perform "housekeeping" tasks like taking attendance and making announcements. Such activities help focus students' attention and help them to begin working quickly and quietly. Quick Tests will function as warm-up exercises. Facts practice could also be used with students (but see the recommended adaptations on page 22.)

the middle of the class period

Keep explanations of new increments very brief.

Next, students should begin a new assignment or correct a returned assignment. Students should refer to their sequence sheets to find the next assignment, whether that be a lesson worksheet, Targeted Practice, Fraction Activity, or test. It is essential that students with learning disabilities complete all the assignments on the sequence sheet in order. If copies have already been made, students may get their own assignments and begin work. Lesson worksheets contain most of the calculation problems from the lessons and clues for solving word problems. As students become more comfortable with the procedures, the clues gradually taper off. **Students must use the lesson worksheets in conjunction with the textbook.**

Students should have no more than two lesson worksheets in their possession at one time—one to complete during the class period and one for homework. (Note that tests should not be assigned as homework.) This will encourage students to complete and correct assignments before moving on.

Explanations to individual students on each new increment should be kept very brief and precise, with the student going directly to the practice portion of the lesson. Use the examples and methodology given on the lesson worksheet. The student should ask for help if the practice is difficult. Most increments can be explained in five minutes or less. (Teaching Hints on specific lesson topics are explained beginning on page 31.)

Students who ask for assistance on only two or three problems in a Written Practice are usually gaining confidence in their ability to work independently. Pointing out information in the *Adaptations Student Reference Guide* during brief tutorials will help students find the information they need in the future.

Notice the reference number in parentheses beneath each numbered problem in the textbook. This number indicates the lesson where the relevant increment was introduced. Encourage students to refer back and reread the explanation of the concept if they need a reminder.

If a student continues to ask for help on more than three problems, it may be necessary to set a limit on the number of "helps" a student may receive per page. This practice will not only push students toward independence, but will also give the teacher a better idea of what a student can actually do. If the student is missing too many problems on independent work, it is time to consider recycling some lessons.

Keep in mind that one-on-one tutoring of students presents a great opportunity for positive reinforcement. Quick, quiet praise for small steps mastered will go a long way toward building self-confidence in mathematics and personal self-esteem.

Students should be encouraged to move forward without the teacher's direction. Strategies presented on the lesson worksheets help students approach new problems. The *Adaptations Student Reference Guide* and the Sequence Sheet foster independence. These tools help students complete assignments and move on quickly to subsequent ones. Students who are absent due to illness may complete assignments at home.

the end of the class period

End each class period with a quick assessment of each student's progress.

Five minutes before the end of the class period, stop students for a quick assessment of the day's progress. A four-week "How to Succeed" chart can be attached to each student's *Adaptations Student Reference Guide*. Ask students to grade themselves daily on items such as completing homework, bringing a pencil to class, demonstrating respect to the teacher and classmates, and completing the required number of assignments. A sample chart is provided on page 16.

Spend the last few minutes of class doing mental math activities, such as those provided in the textbook at the beginning of every lesson. The Mental Math problems in each lesson should be completed orally as a whole-group activity. Choose to focus on one or two useful concepts instead of doing each warm-up in its entirety. *Select carefully what is most useful for the time invested. Avoid getting lost on side trips.* The difficulty of a problem may be adjusted up or down depending on the abilities of individual students. (For example, if a problem asks students to count up by fives from 20, lower-ability students might be asked to begin at 5 instead.) When a series of related problems appears, help the class make connections and discover the pattern.

Sample "How to Succeed" Chart

Name Lucy Smith

"How To Succeed" Chart

Date	Did you complete your homework?	Did you bring a pencil to class?	How many assignments did you do today?
Mon (11/4)	yes	yes	2
Tues (11/5)	yes	yes	2
Wed (11/6)	yes	yes	2
Thurs (11/7)	yes	yes	2
Fri (11/8)	no	yes	1
			No-9 Total 10? **Total**
Mon (11/11)		Holiday	
Tues (11/12)	yes	yes	2
Wed (11/13)	yes	yes	2
Thurs (11/14)	yes	no	2
Fri (11/15)	yes	yes	2
			yes Total 8? **Total**
Mon (11/18)	yes	yes	2
Tues (11/19)	yes	yes	2
Wed (11/20)	yes	yes	2
Thurs (11/21)	yes	yes	2
Fri (11/22)	yes	yes	2
			yes Total 10? **Total**
Mon (11/25)			non-student day
Tues (11/26)			non-student day
Wed (11/27)			Thanksgiving Vacation
Thurs (11/28)			Thanksgiving Vacation
Fri (11/29)			Thanksgiving Vacation
			Total

Homework

Ideally, students will complete two assignments a day, but realistically this is often not possible. Continue to move struggling students along as quickly as possible considering their individual capabilities. Keep in mind that students with special needs must usually make up for lost time. As students progress through the program, they may be able to move at a faster pace.

Students and parents must know that homework will be required daily. Homework is defined as a new lesson, Investigation, Targeted Practice, or Fraction Activity that has not yet been corrected. Using the lesson worksheets, most students can complete assignments in twenty minutes or less; this does not include time to correct mistakes. Thus, in a typical class period students might hand in homework assignments, complete the new classwork assignments, and correct mistakes on their returned homework assignments. The homework that evening would be one of the new assignments that was not completed in class; it might also include correction of the classwork assignment done in class that day. In a five-day week, each student could complete and correct ten assignments. **Please note that tests should never be assigned as homework.**

*Homework is a **daily** requirement. Two assignments per day are recommended for maximum growth.*

Testing

Tests are administered on a regular basis. Each test is cumulative, covering content through a certain lesson. Struggling students tend to require a little more practice with concepts before being tested on them. Thus, it is suggested that tests be given after students have had ten lessons in which to practice the concepts introduced, rather than the five-lesson interval suggested in the textbook. The *Adaptations* testing sequence is shown in the chart on page 20.

It is strongly recommended that calculators **not** be allowed during tests because students need daily review and practice of basic whole number and decimal computation. However, use of the *Adaptations Student Reference Guide* is strongly encouraged. This handy self-help guide will prove itself invaluable as a resource to students who basically know the concepts but need a little support.

It is important to keep in mind as assignments are planned that tests should be completed in class. Individual student assignments for the week can be noted in pencil on the recording form and traced in ink after each assignment is competed, checked, and corrected.

Recycling

Recycling is a process in which students repeat a series of lessons; it is recommended for students who experience difficulty with concepts on the lesson worksheets or tests. Recycling does not hurt the student's grade. Usually it helps the grade because the student will likely grasp missed concepts the second time through. Since students already have some familiarity with the lessons, they can be covered more rapidly.

Beginning with Lesson 15, a test is given after every fifth lesson. If a student performs satisfactorily, he or she should complete the next five lessons. If test results indicate that concept understanding has not been achieved, the student should recycle previous lessons. Recycling is also suggested when a student does poorly on subsequent lesson worksheet assignments.

A sample recording form showing the dot system is shown on page 21.

On lesson worksheets, if a student misses ten or more problems on a problem set on the first attempt, something may be wrong. One suggestion is to make a dot on the recording form the first time this occurs. If the student receives a second dot within the next five days, he or she should recycle back five **lessons preceding the first dot**. (Do **not** use the dot system with Investigations, Targeted Practices, or Fraction Activities.)

On tests, more than five concept errors usually indicates a need for recycling. However, use your judgment with regard to test recycling. If errors are due more to carelessness than to a lack of understanding of concepts, offer students the opportunity to correct errors independently. This will be the most effective way to judge concept mastery.

In summary, use the following recycling guidelines:

- If a student misses **ten or more problems on two lesson worksheets within a five-day period**, recycle the **five lessons preceding the first dot**.

- If a student makes **more than five concept errors on a test**, recycle the **fifteen lessons that precede the test**.

Recycling is beneficial to the struggling student. Even if initially resistant to the idea, the student will eventually appreciate the opportunity for a second chance.

Recycling lessons is beneficial to a struggling student. Even if initially resistant to the idea, the student will eventually appreciate the opportunity for a second chance before moving on to more difficult work. If a student refuses to recycle, give him or her the time and space to calm down and think about the benefits of recycling. The material will be familiar, it will probably take less time to complete, and there will probably be fewer errors to correct. The student should still complete the required number of assignments so the weekly grade will not suffer. (Assigning a bonus point for recycling should help with both attitude and grading.)

Grading

It is recommended that no grades be given for assignments or tests because every assignment should be reworked until all mistakes are corrected. Instead, the recommended grading system is based on how much work a student completes per week. Students may achieve rapid academic growth if they complete eight to ten assignments per week. It is possible to complete five assignments in class and five assignments as homework during a five-day week. Some teachers may choose to make the goal four assignments in class and four assignments as homework, leaving one day free per week for non-routine activities. (Such activities might include computer projects, math-related art or writing projects, hands-on discovery projects, preparation for state assessments, or "catch-up" assignments.)

The recommended grading system is based on how much work a student completes each week.

Each of the following may be considered one assignment:

- A lesson, including practice on a new increment and the Written Practice (i.e., a lesson worksheet);

- An Investigation (because of their length, these may count as two assignments);

- A Targeted Practice or Fraction Activity; or

- A test.

No credit should be given for assignments until all mistakes are corrected. In addition, students must show all of their work; this will help ensure that calculators or other aids have not been used to find the answers. **Because the process of correcting mistakes is so important, it is crucial that someone other than the student check each assignment.**

A sample recording form is shown on page 21.

Weekly grades may be determined by the actual number of assignments that the student completes compared to a weekly goal. For example, if the goal for a week's work is ten assignments, a student who completes and corrects ten assignments during the week would receive an "A" for the week, while a student who completes and corrects seven assignments might receive a "B." The academic level of students in the same classroom my vary by several grade levels, but with this grading scheme it is possible for a student functioning at a 3.5 grade level to get a better grade for the week than a student functioning at a 7.5 grade level. This type of approach emphasizes learning and growth.

Testing Schedule

Lesson Completed	Test Number	Tests Through Lesson...	If Necessary, Recycle Back to Lesson...[†]
15	1	5	1
20	2	10	6
25	3	15	11
30	4	20	16
35	5	25	21
40	6	30	26
45	7	35	31
50	8	40	36
55	9	45	41
60	10	50	46
65	11	55	51
70	12	60	56
75	13	65	61
80	14	70	66
85	15	75	71
90	16	80	76
95	17	85	81
100	18	90	86
105	19	95	91
110	20	100	96
114	21	105	101
117	22	110	106
120	23	115	111

[†] More than five conceptual errors on a test usually indicates a need for recycling. For information on recycling see "Recycling" on page 18.

Sample 10-Assignment Recording Form

Classroom Recording Form   A

Ten Assignments per week

Saxon Math	Attendance					Assignments Completed and Corrected										Grade
Names	M	T	W	TH	F	1	2	3	4	5	6	7	8	9	10	
Katina B.						43	^{TP}43	44	45	T7	46	^{TP}46	47	48	49	
Marloney D.						96	97	98	99	E	100	^{TP}100	T18	101	102	
Johnna P.						26	^{TP}26	27	28	^{TP}28	29	30	T4	31	32	
Jefferson P.						66	B	67	C	68	^{TP}68	69	70	^{TP}70	T12	
Marilyn R.						T1	16	17	18	19	20	T2	•21†	22	•23	
Raven S.						18	19	^{TP}19	20	T2	21	21	22	24	25	
Ralph W.						23	24	25	20	T	21	21			29	
Booker W.						72										
Shameka Y.																
Sarah Y.																
Pierre B.																
Julius D.																
Tyrell G.																
Jori H.																
Zahnda J.																
James J.															17	
Leslie M.										19	20	21	22	24	29	
Jamal M.						81	83	^{TP}84	85	T15	86	^{TP}86	87	88	89	
Jamar P.						99	E	100	^{TP}100	T18	101	102	103	104	105	
Nicole W.						64	65	A	T11	66	B	67	C	68	^{TP}68	
Shaun B.						•101	102	103	•104	69	97	98	99	100	^{TP}100	
Curtis C.						96	97	98	99	E	100	^{TP}100	T18	101	102	
Danny E.						86	^{TP}86	87	88	89	90	^{TP}90	T16	91	92	
Tara N.						46	^{TP}46	47	48	49	50	T8	51	^{TP}51	52	
Emerson M.						85	T15	86	^{TP}86	87	88	89	90	^{TP}90	T16	
Kevin R.						128	1	129	^{TP}29	130	^{TP}130	T24	131	^{TP}131	132	
Edwin S.						60	T10	61	62	^{TP}62	63	^{TP}63	64	65	T11	
John T.						34	35	^{TP}35	T5	36	37	^{TP}37	38	^{TP}38	39	
Joe W.						18	19	^{TP}19	20	T2	21	22	23	24	25	
George W.						29	30	T4	31	32	33	^{TP}33	34	35	^{TP}35	

- Assignments are taken from the sequence sheet.

  Targeted Practice = TP Number (^{TP}55)
  Test = T number (T9)
  Lesson Worksheet = Number (55)
  Fraction Activity = Letter (A)

- Enter assignments for the coming week in pencil to allow changes for students who must recycle.

- As each assignment is completed and corrected, trace over the numbers in ink.

Saxon Math Course 2   SM-7   Adaptations Classroom Recording Form A

†Dots are used to indicate assignments containing ten or more errors. Two or more dots within a five-day period indicate a need for recycling.

An Inclusion Approach

In many school systems, struggling students are taught in the mainstream or inclusion classroom. This approach does not allow for full implementation of the self-paced, individualized *Adaptations* program. Teachers can however help mainstreamed students be successful by using the lesson worksheets, teaching strategies, and extra practice to keep struggling students "on track."

In an inclusion setting, the goal is for all students to progress at the same rate—usually one lesson, investigation, or test per day. Because the number of at-level students will be greater than the number of struggling students, use the instructional model outlined in the Saxon Math Teacher's Manual. This does not mean that all students must receive the same daily instruction or complete every part of the daily lesson; a variety of support mechanisms for struggling students are described in this section. Many of the ideas outlined below will be achieved more easily with the help of a teacher aide or parent volunteer.

power up

The Power Up begins with a Power Up facts practice test. This short, timed exercise builds mastery of fundamental math knowledge that empowers student achievement. Learning basic facts is a significant and genuine accomplishment that can enhance a student's sense of success in and motivation for the subject. Administer the tests as directed in the Saxon Math Teacher's Manual, noting the following exceptions:

- Students with weak visual memory skills will have difficulty memorizing basic math facts. Power Up tests sometimes help, but the gains can be disproportionate to the time and effort spent. This is especially true for students over the age of twelve who are struggling with basic facts. With these students, you may substitute a Quick Test for the Power Up test.

- You may customize the Power Up test to match the needs of students. Memorizing basic facts can be challenging, even daunting for some. Acquiring mastery requires learning a fact or two per day and continually practicing learned facts. Assign only a portion of a Power Up test each day. For instance, all the "times 4" and "times 6" facts one day and all the "times 7" and "times 9" the next. See also Teaching Hint #8 about fact families.

- You may provide alternatives to timed written tests when necessary. While timed tests can stir excitement and motivation for some students, they can also create excessive anxiety for others. In addition some students' Individualized Education Plans disallow timed exams. For such students, you may remove the time restriction or allow them to study flash cards while others complete the facts practice.

Following the Facts Practice is the Mental Math section of the Power Up. The Mental Math problems should be completed orally as a whole-group activity. The difficulty of a problem can be adjusted up or down depending on the abilities of individual students. When selecting a student to answer, let your understanding of who needs practice with individual problems guide you. Try to involve struggling students by asking them questions at their skill level.

The Power Up culminates with Problem Solving. Approach the exercise much like Mental Math, as an oral, whole-group activity. Let students share ideas and collaborate to derive the answer. If students are stumped by a problem, suggest that they try a different strategy.

Keep these Power Up activities brief. Try to complete all three in fifteen minutes or less. They are intended to energize students' minds for math and establish a tempo for the remaining portions of the lesson.

lesson worksheets

Lesson worksheets must be used in conjunction with the Student Edition.

The simplest adaptation for the lesson is to allow struggling students to use the lesson worksheets and the *Adaptations Student Reference Guide*. Each lesson worksheet summarizes the lesson by highlighting key facts, examples, and procedures. Because the lesson summaries are brief, students are more likely to read them. Reliance on simpler language, and sometimes simplified methods, ensures that more students will understand and remember the concepts.

The lesson worksheets' greatest value is the support they provide for Written Practice problems, including:

- identifying a starting point;
- restating the problem;
- crafting a partial solution;
- citing an *Adaptations Student Reference Guide* page;
- referring students to a page in the textbook; and
- reminding students to include units in the answer.

new concept

Incorporate the examples on the lesson worksheets when applying whole-group instruction.

The New Concept portion of the lesson presents new instruction and should usually take five to ten minutes. Use the following ideas to address the needs of struggling students:

- While the textbook might provide several examples to demonstrate the new concept, only one or two of those will be shown on the lesson worksheet. Be especially mindful of those examples, and plan your instruction around them.
- Avoid wordiness and complexity.

*Enhance instruction with the **Adaptations Student Reference Guide**, lesson worksheets, Teaching Guide, and manipulatives.*

Struggling students should follow along in the textbook first, and then go over the simplified and condensed instruction on the lesson worksheet. At this point it is very helpful for the teacher or an aide to guide the student through the summary section of the lesson worksheet, including:

- pointing out charts in the *Adaptations Student Reference Guide*, especially on introduction of a new chart;
- using the Teaching Hints from this guide (beginning on page 33). They discuss alternate teaching strategies and help prevent stumbling blocks; and
- incorporating manipulatives and visuals into the instruction.

practice set

The Practice Set usually contains five to ten problems focusing on the day's topics. The lesson worksheet provides the full text of most problems and sets up many of the solutions, giving more help at first and gradually reducing assistance throughout.

Solve the first few problems in the Practice Set as a class; then have students complete the remaining problems on their own or in small groups. The problems on the lesson worksheet are identical to the problems in the textbook, so lesson worksheet use is no hindrance to group activity. You will, however, have to monitor that students who do not need the "helps" provided by the lesson worksheets are not using them.

written practice

Reserve most of the math period for Written Practice.

After students complete the Practice Set, they should move directly into the Written Practice and work on the problems individually. Ideally, students will spend most of the class period on Written Practice. Use the following suggestions to enhance the learning opportunity that the Mixed Practice provides:

- Help students learn how to be resourceful problem solvers by teaching them how to use the materials that will improve their understanding of concepts (*Adaptations Student Reference Guide*, charts, manipulatives, textbook). Ensure easy access to manipulatives and other resources.

- Point out the lesson reference numbers shown in parentheses under the problem numbers in the textbook. Each one identifies a lesson that students can review if they have forgotten how to solve the corresponding problem. Rereading lessons or reviewing examples may refresh students' memories.

- Circulate through the classroom and provide one-on-one help as needed. If multiple students need help at the same time, instruct students to work on more familiar problems until you or a teaching assistant can help them.

supplemental practice

Extra practice can benefit struggling students and at-level students having difficulty with a specific topic.

Extra practice can be assigned as classwork or homework to struggling students (or at-level students who are having difficulty with a specific topic). Targeted Practice and Fraction Activity worksheets provide one to two pages of problems on a single topic. Assigning a bonus point for completion will encourage students to complete the extra work. Use your knowledge of individual students' abilities when giving extra practice. See the charts of topics covered by Targeted Practice and Fraction Activities beginning on page 80. (The Fraction Activities are designed to be completed with fraction manipulatives, so ensure that students have their own sets before assigning as homework.)

tests

Testing tips:
- *Strongly discourage calculator use (except with physically disabled students).*
- *Encourage reference guide use.*
- *Test in class only.*

Tests are administered on a regular basis and are cumulative, covering content through a certain lesson. Concepts are assessed only after they have been practiced in at least five Written Practices.

The cumulative nature of the tests, the testing schedule, and the additional activities on test day can pose difficulties for some students. To ensure success, you can make a number of adjustments to the normal routine:

- Allow students to use adapted test worksheets. Much like lesson worksheets, they provide support for solving individual problems, including the full text of every problem, workspace, answer boxes, and hints for select problems.

- Encourage students to use their *Adaptations Student Reference Guide* as a resource during the exam.

- If recent performance suggests students will struggle with their next test, delay the exam to allow more practice time. The testing schedule on page 20 allows students to practice concepts for ten Written Practices before assessing the material.

- Distribute tests from a common folder or bundle to avoid stigmatizing students who are using the *Adaptations* program or who are on an alternate testing schedule.

Cumulative Tests are the best indicators of whether students have misunderstandings. Scores below 80 percent usually signal the need for remediation. The Test-Item Analyses allow you to analyze individual students' performances. They identify the concepts of each test problem and the lessons that introduce them. If a student performs poorly on a test, compare his or her exam to its corresponding Test-Item Analysis, placing a check mark beside every problem answered incorrectly.

Next compare the checked items. Are they on related topics? If so, the student might need to be retaught those topics. Are the lessons for the checked items clustered? If so, the student might need more practice on that section of lessons. Analyzing consecutive tests may provide deeper insight into a student's strengths and weaknesses.

decreasing usage of support materials

If allowed to choose, students will often discontinue their use of lesson worksheets at the appropriate time.

Some students will be able to transition away from using *Adaptations* materials partway through the school year. Use the following practices to facilitate the change:

- Throughout the year, make lesson worksheet use optional. Many students will elect to move away from them on their own. (Note: You might have to monitor this as a few students will attempt the transition too soon.)

- Do not allow capable students to use the lesson worksheets as a "crutch."

- Gradually reduce students' use of lesson worksheets. Let students try one lesson without the corresponding worksheet. Students who score 80 percent or better can complete the next lesson the same way. Students who score below 80 percent can try again in a couple of weeks.

- Remind students throughout the year that they will not be able to use reference guides on end-of-year standardized exams. In early spring, begin impressing upon students the need to cut back their use of reference guides on tests. Most students will do so on their own.

- Use the answer forms from the Instructional Masters for students to use as they transition from lesson worksheets to notebook paper. Answer forms establish a workspace for each problem but do not contain the helps found on lesson worksheets.

Not all students should transition away from using *Adaptations* materials. Continue to use the materials with students who consistently function below their target grade level.

Teaching English Language Learners

English-language learners in an inclusion classroom should participate in the daily lesson. Whenever possible, use manipulatives and refer to posters and diagrams to illustrate concepts and vocabulary in the lesson. Visual cues will make the words you are saying more clear.

It is of paramount importance that English-language learners feel comfortable participating in class. If students seem reluctant to respond to questions in English, give them non-verbal ways to answer, such as giving a thumbs-up, clapping, or writing answers on the board. Avoid correcting their grammar if they make mistakes. Instead, model correct grammar by affirming their statements and restating them correctly. Foster an atmosphere in your classroom where native English speakers are respectful of English-language learners and where English-language learners are given opportunities to interact and participate fully with their native English speaking peers.

Foster an atmosphere in your classroom where native English speakers are respectful of English-language learners and where English-language learners are given opportunities to interact and participate fully with their native English speaking peers.

After the lesson, provide English-language learners with a lesson worksheet and *Adaptations Student Reference Guide*. English-language learners may find the worksheets included in the adaptation useful, since they contain simpler language than the textbook. They also contain bolded words that call students' attention to important vocabulary. The *Adaptations Student Reference Guide* has charts that list important vocabulary and keywords and help with spellings.

English-language learners will benefit from working in pairs or small groups. You may want to pair students with native English speakers or speakers at more advanced levels of English speaking ability. These students can help other English-language learners gain valuable experience speaking English. Be sure to monitor students closely to ensure that all the students in the pairs and small groups are participating. One way to ensure participation is to assign roles such as recorder, reporter, and supplies person. These roles should have specific and equally important responsibilities. Be sure to rotate roles so that students get to experience each one.

If you have more than one ESL student from the same language background, encourage those students to discuss the day's lesson in their native language. If students can process and clarify the concept in their native language, they may be better able to transfer that knowledge into English.

Classroom Management

Early in the school year, establish a consistent classroom procedure that allows students to leave their seats to turn in assignments and to get materials they need to continue working. Prevention of problems is the key. To help achieve this goal:

- Store lesson worksheets in a location easily accessible to the students.

- Establish a route for students to move around the classroom without disturbing the class.

- Store manipulatives in a location easily accessible to the students.

- Use boxes labeled "Work to be corrected" and "Work that's been corrected."

- Instruct students to work on easier problems while waiting for help on more difficult ones.

- If you use self-paced instruction, direct students to begin the next assignment while they wait to receive an assignment that they might need help to correct.

- Designate someone to act as a helper if you are interrupted or called to the door for a conference.

- Establish a three-step plan for handling disruptive behavior (for example, verbal warning, time out, and detention).

Establish a consistent classroom procedure as soon as possible. Prevention of problems is key.

classroom aides

In many classrooms, effectively using class time while meeting individual instructional needs is more easily achieved with the assistance of classroom aides (paraprofessionals, teaching assistants, parent volunteers, or students earning elective credits). Classroom aides free you to:

- give one-on-one instruction of new increments;

- respond quickly to students who ask for help;

- teach appropriate classroom behavior privately;

- have regular, quiet, personal interaction with each student;

- work on positive, continual reinforcement.

The ideal student classroom aides are those who have completed at least one year of Saxon Math and have proven themselves to be accurate and reliable. These students can be assigned to help others.

Adult assistants or parent volunteers can supervise the student classroom aides, keep records, prepare materials for future assignments, help answer students' questions, alert you to potential problems with students' understanding, and return papers to students. (Note: Local privacy laws might limit the kinds of tasks parent volunteers may perform.) It is recommended that adults perform the more sensitive, managerial tasks and that students be limited to helping with supplies and assisting other students with simple tasks. With efficient classroom aides, you are free to concentrate on meeting individual learning needs.

motivation

Always teach as if the student were your own child. How will they feel about themselves at the end of the school day? We all know that children respond better to positive reinforcement, but it is easy to slip into negative thinking. Remember that little things make a lot of difference.

Daily verbal encouragement and positive remarks on graded papers are extremely important to student success. It is amazing how a little shared humor or a reminder of a previous achievement can brighten a student's outlook.

Take the time to recognize small successes. When a student can finally tell you with ease that four-thirds equals one and one-third, rejoice. This is a breakthrough and the student needs to know it. Remind the student how he or she struggled with this concept only last week. The student needs to know that future struggles will become easier in time. This is called *hope*.

Motivational tips:
- *Provide daily encouragement.*
- *Recognize small successes.*
- *Mark papers with the number of problems worked correctly.*

Reward struggling students for completing and correcting all assignments for the week with a certificate, a pencil, or a small snack. Completing a textbook is a particularly important achievement and should be marked with a small celebration and recognition from the school principal.

Using red ink to check assignments has a negative effect on student morale. Blue and green are better choices. In addition, mark papers with the number of problems worked correctly rather than the number missed.

When a student begins demonstrating acting-out behavior or passive resistance, that student is probably being asked to do something that is too hard for him or her at the time. The teacher needs to go back and see where the learning broke down. The student needs another chance to go back and master the concept that isn't fully in place. Usually when a student *can* do the work, he or she *will* do the work.

Provide a soothing learning environment. Soft classical music with 60 beats per minute has shown in repeated studies to increase both the long-term and short-term memory of the task at hand. Subjects such as math and languages can be retained better when coupled with music that matches the heartbeat, but does not have a distracting melody. Try playing "Pachelbel's Canon" softly in the background. A nice side effect is the calming effect the music will have.

involving parents	Daily assignments are essential for struggling students. Parents should be alerted that homework will be a common occurrence in their child's math education. If homework is not completed, the student will not progress, and his or her grade will suffer. If poor homework habits occur on a regular basis, contact the parents to determine the cause. Call home to share good news as well.
rule for success	Students with difficulties will be more likely to succeed in Saxon Math Course 2 if:

- **they complete the lessons in sequence.** The problem sets have been carefully crafted to provide continual practice and review of all the concepts, processes, and procedures introduced since the first lesson. Students must complete all the problems in each problem set, and the lessons must be completed in sequence.

- **they correct all errors in the lessons.** Because a problem that is missed in one lesson will reappear in another form in subsequent lessons, students must correct their own mistakes to be successful.

- **they complete homework assignments.** Homework is essential. It develops appropriate study habits and makes it possible to close the gap between students' functional level and target grade level.

- **they compete tests in class.** Tests provide you with the information needed to diagnose whether students have mastered the material.

- **calculator use is limited.** As a general rule, calculators should not be used unless special individual circumstances warrant otherwise. Mathematical skills are maintained through practice in whole-number and decimal calculations. Also, students demonstrate understanding by showing all the steps required in working problems. Students may use calculators at the teacher's discretion, but students should still work out all problems in the lessons. Calculators should not be allowed during tests.

- **positive reinforcement is used.** Provide continual, positive reinforcement for students' achievements, large and small. With each success, students will gain more confidence and will be more likely to meet future challenges in the mathematics classroom and in other academic areas with positive attitudes and feeling of competence. Students will soon learn to expect success, and their improved self-images will lead to greater effectiveness.

- **different teaching approaches are used.** Because students learn in a variety of ways, use varied approaches to the same concept to reach the greatest number of students. For auditory learners, orally explain concepts as clearly as possible. For visual learners, employ visual aids such as charts, diagrams, and the *Adaptations Student Reference Guide*. For kinesthetic learners, have manipulatives readily available.

Teaching Strategies

Struggling students need brief, specific directions. The following teaching strategies will help explain new concepts simply and easily.

Struggling students need brief, specific directions with supporting visuals and manipulatives. The following pages contain detailed teaching strategies and techniques to use when introducing new concepts. These strategies, called Teaching Hints in this guide, are identified by number and are referenced on the lesson worksheets at point of use. The table below identifies the appropriate lesson or investigation (Inv.) in which to introduce each hint; the hints are discussed beginning on page 33.

Hint	Concept	Introduce in Lesson...	Teaching Guide Page
1	Regrouping Across Zeros	TP1A	33
2	Offset Multiplication	TP1B	33
3	Multiplication by Two Digits	TP1B	34
4	Ways to Show Division	TP1C	35
5	Short Division	TP1C	36
6	Long Division	TP1C	37
7	Column Addition (Sets of Ten)	1	38
8	Fact Families	2	39
9	Long Division: "Canceling Matching Zeros"	2	40
10	Finding Missing Numbers	3	41
11	Positive and Negative Numbers	4	42
12	Comparing Numbers	4	42
13	Finding Patterns in Sequences	4	43
14	Abbreviations and Symbols	4	44
15	Place Value (Digit Lines)	5	45
16	Factors of Whole Numbers	6	46
17	Finding the Greatest Common Factor	6	46
18	Tests for Divisibility	6	47
19	Geometry Vocabulary	7	48
20	Naming Fractions/Identifying Fractional Parts	8	49
21	Fraction Manipulatives	8	49
22	Percent	8	51
23	Reading Inch Rulers	8	51
24	Reciprocal	9	52
25	Improper Fractions	10	52
26	Word Problem Cues	11	53
27	Rate	13	53

Hint	Concept	Introduce in Lesson...	Teaching Guide Page
28	Finding the Missing Part	14	55
29	Probability	14	56
30	Canceling Fractions	15	56
31	Measuring Liquids and Capacities of Containers	16	57
32	Area and Perimeter Vocabulary	19	58
33	Perimeter of Complex Shapes	19	59
34	Square Roots	20	60
35	Prime Factorization Using the Factor Tree	21	60
36	Prime Factorization Using Division by Primes	21	61
37	Prime Factorization of Powers of Ten	21	61
38	Finding Square Roots Using Prime Factorization	21	62
39	Fraction of a Group	22	62
40	Finding the Least Common Multiple	27	64
41	Average	28	64
42	Estimating or Rounding	29	65
43	Comparing Fractions	30	65
44	Rectangular Coordinates	Inv. 3	66
45	Coordinate Geometry	Inv. 3	67
46	Decimal Place Value (Digit Lines)	31	67
47	Writing Numbers	31	68
48	Tenths and Hundredths	31	69
49	Reading Metric Rulers	32	69
50	Gram/Kilogram Manipulatives	32	70
51	Decimal Arithmetic Reminders Chart	35	71
52	Complex Average	55	71
53	Classifying Quadrilaterals	Inv. 6	72
54	Geometric Solids (Manipulatives)	67	73
55	Faces on a Cube	67	73
56	Surface Area of a Prism	67	74
57	Volume	70	75
58	Proportion Setups	97	76
59	Scale Factor	98	77
60	Comparing Volume	113	79

Teaching Hints

how to use hints 1-6

Hints 1-6 are not linked to a specific lesson but are included for students who struggle with working certain types of mathematical problems that are not covered in *Saxon Math Course 2*.

- If a student is having trouble regrouping numbers with zeros, review Hint #1: Regrouping Across Zeros and assign TP 1A.

- If a student is having trouble multiplying by numbers ending in zeros, review Hint #2: Offset Multiplication and assign TP 1B.

- If a student is having trouble multiplying by numbers with two digits, review Hint #3: Multiplication by Two Digits and assign TP 1B.

- If a student is having trouble understanding the different forms of division or differentiating among dividend, divisor, and quotient, review Hint #4: Ways to Show Division and assign TP 1C.

- If a student is having trouble dividing by a one-digit number, review Hint #5: Short Division and assign TP 1C.

- If a student is having trouble dividing by a two-digit number, review Hint #6: Long Division and assign TP 1C.

Hint #1: regrouping across zeros

(Introduce in Targeted Practice 1A)

*Remember the phrase "Borrow across **all zeros**."*

Students tend to get lost when they regroup one step at a time (as many were taught to do in earlier grades). A simpler method is to borrow across all the consecutive zeros, and then subtract. Students can usually grasp this process quickly and are far more accurate in their computations. (In money problems, ignore the decimal point when borrowing.)

$$
\begin{array}{r}
{}^{2\,9\,9_{1}}\!\!\!\!\!\!\!\!\!\!\!\!\!\!\!\!\not{3}\not{0}\not{0}1 \\
-\,1322 \\
\hline
1679
\end{array}
\qquad
\begin{array}{r}
{}^{3\,9_{1}}\!\!\!\!\!\!\!\!\!\!\!\not{4}\not{0}6 \\
-\,159 \\
\hline
247
\end{array}
\qquad
\begin{array}{r}
{}^{4\;\;9_{1}}\!\!\!\!\!\!\!\!\!\!\!\$5.\not{0}0 \\
-\,\$2.34 \\
\hline
\$2.66
\end{array}
$$

For the example on the left above, say the following:

"I can't take two from one, so I'll borrow one from 300. This leaves 299. The one I borrowed goes here and becomes eleven. Now I'll subtract as usual."

Hint #2: offset multiplication

(Introduce in Targeted Practice 1B)

Teach students to write zeros "hanging out" to the right.

Offset multiplication is a common method of multiplying a number and a multiple of 10, 100, or 1000. Many students will already be familiar with the concept, but it is worthwhile to teach this shortcut to those students who are not:

1. Write the nonzero number on top.
2. Write the zero number "hanging out."
3. Rewrite the "hanging out" zeros in the answer.
4. Then multiply the remaining digits.

Example: 2000×34

$$
\begin{array}{r}
34 \\
\times\,2\,000 \\
\hline
68{,}000
\end{array}
$$

Hint #3:
multiplication by two digits
(Introduce in Targetd Practice 1B)

When multiplying by two digits, visualize the two-digit multiplier as two one-digit multipliers.

Multiplication by two digits is difficult for students who have difficulty with sequencing or visual perception. Although most students will be able to multiply two digits by one digit with proficiency by now, many will get confused when multiplying two digits by two digits. The following procedure was developed by a student who also experienced these difficulties.

Visualize the two-digit multiplier as two one-digit multipliers. When finished multiplying by the "first" digit, cross it out; then place an *X* on the second line of multiplication as a reminder to indent. (Using zeros as placeholders is less effective, since students may confuse the placeholders with problem numbers.)

For the problem 34 × 12, the procedure can be summarized in four steps:

1. Multiply by the ones digit (ignore the tens digit):

$$\begin{array}{r} 34 \\ \times\ 12 \\ \hline 68 \end{array}$$

2. Cross out the 2 when you are finished with it:

$$\begin{array}{r} 34 \\ \times\ 1\cancel{2} \\ \hline 68 \end{array}$$

3. Indent the next line using *x* as a placeholder. Multiply by the tens digit:

$$\begin{array}{r} 3\ 4 \\ \times\ 1\ \cancel{2} \\ \hline 6\ 8 \\ +\ 3\ 4\ x \\ \hline \end{array}$$

4. Add the two answers:

$$\begin{array}{r} 3\ 4 \\ \times\ 1\ \cancel{2} \\ \hline 6\ 8 \\ +\ 3\ 4\ x \\ \hline 4\ 0\ 8 \end{array}$$

Graph paper can be used as a visual aid to line up columns and rows.

On problems involving money, it may be necessary to remind students to write dollar signs and decimal points in their final answers.

Hint #4:

ways to show division

(Introduce in Targeted Practice 1C)

Teach students to locate the dividend and to say the dividend first when reading a division problem.

Students often have trouble with the various ways of showing division, largely because they do not understand the concept thoroughly. Many students simply do not hear any difference between "twenty-four divided by six" and "six divided by twenty-four." This is especially true of students who are not developmentally ready to grasp the abstract nature of division. Therefore, when students were first taught division, although it was certainly not mathematically pure, they were taught to say the greater number first. This idea, coupled with repeated oral and written practice of the various ways to write "twenty-four divided by six," was often the best way to instill the concept of division.

Example: *"Say the **greater** number (dividend) **FIRST**."*

"twenty-four divided by six" $\quad 6\overline{)24} \quad\quad 24 \div 6 \quad\quad \dfrac{24}{6}$

Now, because students in *Saxon Math Course 2* have been practicing division problems for several years, they are ready to be taught that division problems are read as "the **dividend** divided by the **divisor** equals the quotient." Since students may now be required to compute "one divided by two" where the dividend is no longer the greater number, teach them to locate the dividend and to always say the dividend (not the greater number) first.

The chart below is located on page 5 in the *Adaptations Student Reference Guide.*

Division

Three ways to show division:

$$divisor \overline{)\,\textbf{dividend}}^{\;quotient}$$

$$\dfrac{\textbf{dividend}}{divisor} = quotient$$

$$\textbf{dividend} \div divisor = quotient$$

Example: "Twelve divided by four equals three."

$$4\overline{)12}^{\;3} \quad\quad \dfrac{12}{4} = 3 \quad\quad 12 \div 4 = 3$$

Say the larger number (dividend) first.

Hint #5:
short division
(Introduce in Targeted Practice 1C)

Teaching students short division will also help improve their mental math abilities.

Students frequently get lost in the steps of long division. Although they will need to work all the steps with multidigit divisors, they will be more confident if they have learned to use short division with single-digit divisors.

Take time to teach the short division method described below. Students who have struggled with long division may resist the idea at first, but most will eventually like the new method because it is so much easier. An additional benefit is an improvement in students' ability to do mental math.

The rules of short division are simple:

- Any number "left over" goes in front of the next digit.

- Any final number "left over" becomes the remainder. (Remainders must be smaller than divisors.)

- There must be one digit in the quotient above each digit in the dividend. A cue for thus rule is *"Digit above each digit."*

- If necessary, have students use zero as a placeholder.[†] (If the divisor won't divide into the first digit of the dividend, place a small zero above that digit.)

For example, when giving the problem below, simply remind students that after multiplying and subtracting, the "leftover" goes in front of the next digit.

$$2\ 9$$
$$3\overline{)8^2 7}$$

Remind students to place a digit above each digit and to use zero as a placeholder. You can also help students visualize the process by circling the first two digits of the dividend (when appropriate).

$$_0 7\ 8 \qquad _0 7\ 8\ R\ 1$$
$$3\overline{)\textcircled{23}^2 4} \qquad 3\overline{)\textcircled{23}^2 5}$$

Insist that students use short division—do not allow the use of long division for single-digit divisors. One reason to insist on short division is that students often have a difficult time lining up numbers correctly in long division. This becomes a stumbling block to the concept of division. Students will cope better with long division if they have confidence in short division.

[†] It may be necessary to remind students to remove initial placeholder zeros when writing their final answers.

Hint #6:
long division
(Introduce in Targeted Practice 1C)

To make long division easier:
- *Use zero as a placeholder.*
- *Place a digit above each digit.*

With two-digit divisors, use long division. (This is the conventional method of "divide, multiply, subtract, and bring down.") Although the sequencing and visual perception demands of long division may be difficult for some students, two things will make the process a little easier and thus more accurate.

First, continue to use zero as a placeholder.[†] Second, remember that there must be a digit in the quotient above each digit in the dividend, including any zeros used as placeholders. Thus, a three-digit dividend must have a three-digit quotient.

The rules may be summarized as follows:

- Use **long division** with **two-digit divisors.** (Continue to use short division with one-digit divisors.)

- "Divide, multiply, subtract, and bring down."

- Use zero as a placeholder.

- Place a digit above each digit.

- Make sure any remainder is smaller than the divisor.

$$\begin{array}{r} {}_0 3\,4\text{ R }2 \\ 10\overline{)34\,2} \\ -30 \\ \hline 4\,2 \\ -4\,0 \\ \hline 2 \end{array}$$

Help students make educated guesses during long division. Once the placeholder zero(s) is inserted, ask students to round **down** the divisor to the nearest multiple of ten before making the first "guess."

Example: $32\overline{)128}$ (Think: $30\overline{)120}$)

This is the most difficult level in the entire process of teaching division. Reassure students that understanding will come. If the process continues to be a stumbling block, practice more division by multiples of ten. Then practice rounding down divisors that are **not** multiples of ten. Students must become comfortable doing this before they attempt the far more difficult task of "rounding up."

[†] It may be necessary to remind students to remove initial placeholder zeros when writing their final answers.

Hint #7:
column addition (sets of ten)
(Introduce in Lesson 1)

Students who lack facility with number facts have trouble with column addition. A shortcut is to cross off the sets of ten in the ones column, keeping track of the sets with the fingers of one hand. When all the sets of ten have been found, add the remaining digits and combine this number with the sets of ten. Carry, and then repeat the process with the tens column, the hundreds column, etc.

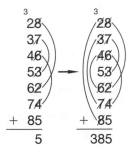

A "Sets of Ten" chart helps students remember the possible combinations of ten.

For the beginning lessons, it helps to provide a chart of the possible combinations of ten on the board, on the wall, or in an empty area of the *Adaptations Student Reference Guide.* **Remind students periodically to cross off sets of ten.** Without a reminder, many will forget to cross off sets of ten and simply continue their slow, self-defeating habits.

Sets of Ten

9 + 1 = 10
8 + 2 = 10
7 + 3 = 10
6 + 4 = 10
5 + 5 = 10

Hint #8:
fact families
(Introduce in Lesson 2)

Pointing out that only a finite number of facts must be learned makes it easier for students to learn those facts.

Students who have difficulty remembering number facts may be overwhelmed by the number of them to be learned. Two things will make this simpler. First, when a relationship of three numbers is shown, the facts are much easier to remember. Second, when students realize only a finite number of facts must be learned, their confidence that they can learn those facts increases. Use the following dialogue to introduce addition/subtraction fact families:

"The numbers 5, 6, and 11 form a fact family. Write two addition and two subtraction facts using these three numbers."

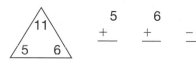

*"If you know one fact family, you know **four** facts."*

5 + 6 = 11	11 − 5 = 6
6 + 5 = 11	11 − 6 = 5

The following dialogue may be helpful when introducing multiplication/division fact families:

"Any number times zero equals zero."

"Any number times one equals itself."

"Everybody seems to know their 2's and 5's facts."

"These are the only facts left to learn."

Triangle fact cards such as the ones shown here are included in the Adaptation Manipulative Kit.

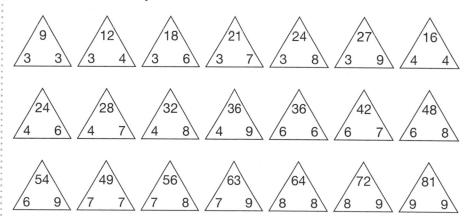

*"If you know one fact family, you know **four** facts."*

3 × 9 = 27	27 ÷ 3 = 9
9 × 3 = 27	27 ÷ 9 = 3

A hint to make long division easier is to remove an ending zero from both the divisor and the dividend before dividing, thus making it possible to use short division.[†] Removing the ending zeros is simply a short form of reducing by dividing the dividend and divisor by ten or "canceling matching zeros." Learning to use the procedure now will help students when they reach lessons where the procedure becomes a necessity. The steps are as follows:

1. Rewrite the problem in fractional form.
   (This may be only a mental step.)

2. Reduce the fraction by dividing both terms by 10.
   (**"Cancel matching zeros."**)

3. Use short division.

$$20\overline{)1340} \quad \longrightarrow \quad \frac{134\cancel{0}}{2\cancel{0}} \quad \longrightarrow \quad {}_{0}6\,7 \atop 2\overline{)13^14}$$

If the quotient is to be written as a whole number, a decimal number, or a mixed number, no alteration of the answer is necessary. However, if the answer has a remainder, the students must add the zero "back" to the remainder. Thus:

$$40\overline{)2790}^{\,\text{R}} \quad \longrightarrow \quad \frac{279\cancel{0}}{4\cancel{0}} \quad \longrightarrow \quad {}_{0}6\,9\,\text{R3} \atop 4\overline{)27^39} \quad \text{so} \quad {}_{0\,0}69\,\text{R30} \atop 40\overline{)27^390}$$

[†]This procedure cannot be used with money amounts or with digits other than zero.

Finding missing numbers requires a somewhat sophisticated type of thinking. For some students, the procedure may be visualized by giving examples such as the following:

> *"You have some cookies in your hand. I take three away, and you have two left. How many cookies did you start with? First decide if the amount you started with was* **more** *or* **less** *than three. If it was* **more**, *we* **add**. *If it was* **less**, *we* **subtract**."*

Students will associate the words *more* with add and *less* with subtract, enabling them to solve the problem.

> *"Was the amount you started with more or less than three?"* (more)

> *"Then we add. 3 + 2 = 5. You started with five cookies."*

Other students cannot perform the missing number calculations unless they use the "Missing Numbers" chart on page 4 in the *Adaptations Student Reference Guide* (and below). Usually, with enough practice using this chart, students will internalize the concepts and no longer need to look them up. The most important part of this chart is the two-part subtraction rule.

The most important part of the "Missing Numbers" chart is the two-part subtraction rule.

Missing Numbers	
Operation	Examples
Addition: To find the missing **addend** → **subtract**	$\begin{array}{r}2\\+A\\\hline5\end{array}$ $\begin{array}{r}5\\-2\\\hline A\end{array}=3$ $\qquad$ $\begin{array}{r}B\\+3\\\hline5\end{array}$ $\begin{array}{r}5\\-3\\\hline B\end{array}=2$
Subtraction: 1. To find the missing **top** number (minuend) → **add** 2. To find the missing **bottom** number (subtrahend) → **subtract**	$\begin{array}{r}N\\-3\\\hline2\end{array}$ $\begin{array}{r}3\\+2\\\hline N\end{array}=5$ $\begin{array}{r}5\\-Y\\\hline2\end{array}$ $\begin{array}{r}5\\-2\\\hline Y\end{array}=3$
Multiplication: To find the missing **factor** → **divide**	$\begin{array}{r}3\\\times N\\\hline6\end{array}$ $N=2$ $3\overline{)6}$ $\qquad$ $\begin{array}{r}N\\\times 2\\\hline6\end{array}$ $N=3$ $2\overline{)6}$
Division: 1. To find the missing **dividend** → **multiply** 2. To find the missing **divisor** → **divide**	$2\overline{)N}$ $\begin{array}{r}8\\\times 2\\\hline N\end{array}=16$ $N\overline{)8}$ $\begin{array}{r}N=4\\2\overline{)8}\end{array}$

Hint #11:
positive and negative numbers
(Introduce in Lesson 4)

A discussion of negative numbers in terms of below-zero temperatures will be effective in areas where winter temperatures drop below zero. Use the following dialogue:

> *"At 8 a.m. the thermometer read 8° Celsius. By 9 a.m., as the storm passed through, the temperature had dropped 10°. How cold was it at 9 a.m.?"*

Students will also find it helpful to have a number line showing positive and negative numbers that they can work with. When teaching the addition of numbers on a number line, instruct students to always begin the problem (not each addend) at the origin.

See "Number Line" on page 9 in the *Adaptations Student Reference Guide*.

Hint #12:
comparing numbers
(Introduce in Lesson 4)

Teach students that the "big" (or "open") end points to the bigger number, and vice versa.

Students may need memory cues to remember the symbols for "less than" ($<$) and "greater than" ($>$). Since each symbol has a "big" end and a "little" end, demonstrate that the "big" (or "open") end points to the bigger number and vice versa. Some visual learners may benefit from drawing a graphic such as a "hungry alligator" whose mouth opens up to "eat the bigger number."

Less Than/Greater Than	
15 < 50	50 > 15
little < big	big > little

Hint #13:
finding patterns in sequences

(Introduce in Lesson 4)

Finding the pattern in a sequence is an automatic task for most students, but students who have little or no facility with numbers must be shown the strategy. Sequences are fairly simple to find using the "Multiplication Table" on page 3 in the *Adaptations Student Reference Guide*. Knowing which row or column to use, however, is more difficult.

A simple procedure is to subtract any two adjacent numbers in the sequence. Once this difference is found, locate that number's row or column (it does not matter which) in the table. Then determine whether the numbers in the pattern increase or decrease, and fill in the missing numbers. For example, with the problem below, the following dialogue might be used:

"Find the next three numbers in this sequence."

... , 24, 20, 16, _____, _____, _____, ...

"Look at the pattern and find the difference between the first two numbers."   (24 − 20 = 4)

"Now find the Multiplication Table in your Adaptations Student Reference Guide.*"*

"Look at the '4's' row (or column) in the Multiplication Table."

"Do the numbers in the sequence increase or decrease?" (decrease)

"What is the pattern?"   (subtract 4)

"What are the next three numbers?"   (12, 8, 4)

For other types of sequences, teach students how to inspect the numbers to discover the rule. Ask "What is done to each number to make the next number?" A cue for this procedure is "Find the pattern. Continue it."

Teach students how to inspect the numbers to discover the rule. A cue for this procedure is "Find the pattern. Continue it."

$$\overset{+4}{\frown}\ \overset{-1}{\frown}\ \overset{+4}{\frown}\ \overset{-1}{\frown}\ \overset{+4}{\frown}$$

3,   7,   6,   10,   9,   13, . . .

Some common math abbreviations and symbols are used throughtout the *Saxon Math Course 2* textbook.

approximately equals	≈		mile	mi
centimeter	cm		milliliter	mL
degree Celsius	°C		millimeter	mm
degree Fahrenheit	°F		minute	min
foot	ft		ounce	oz
gallon	gal		pi	π
hour	hr		point	pt
inch	in.		pound	lb
kilogram	kg		quart	qt
kilometer	km		second	s
liter	L		yard	yd
meter	m		year	yr

Remind students that units are part of the answer.

The answers to some problems use a slightly different form or a combination of abbreviations. Alert students to the different ways these abbreviations may be used. Students may need to be reminded that the units are actually part of the answer. Some examples follow:

Lesson 20   area[†] expressed in square units
$in.^2$, *sq. in., square inches;* ft^2, *sq. ft, square feet*

Investigation 3   length and perimeter on the coordinate plane
units

area on the coordinate plane
units²

Lesson 46   miles per hour
mph, $\frac{miles}{hour}$, $\frac{mi}{hr}$

kilometers per hour

$\frac{km}{hr}$

miles per gallon

mpg, $\frac{miles}{gallon}$, $\frac{mi}{gal}$

Lesson 70   volume[†] expressed in cubic units
$in.^3$, *cu. in., cubic inches;*
cm^3, *cu. cm, cubic centimeters*

[†] Remind students that units of area and volume are often written with exponents. It may be helpful to point out the relationship between the number of factors and the exponent in the answer. Area is found by multiplying two dimensions and can be written with an exponent of 2. Volume is found by multiplying three dimensions and can be written with an exponent of 3.

place value (digit lines)

(Introduce in Lesson 5)

Teach students to discover the pattern in reading numbers.

Once students discover the pattern of place value, it makes reading and writing numbers much simpler. Point out the "Place Value" chart on page 11 in the *Adaptations Student Reference Guide*. Call attention to the obvious groups of three digits separated by commas. If we call these groups families, each family has a different last name: the units family, the thousands family, the millions family, etc. Every family has only three members: ones, tens, and hundreds. Commas separate the three-digit families. Starting with the thousands family, we always give the family name to the comma following the family. Point out that the units family does not have a comma. Drawing a circle around each "family" helps to visualize this idea.

$$(347) , (628) , (407)$$

Ask students to read only the circled 347. Now ask them to identify the family by the comma. Next have them read the circled 628. Identify the family by the comma. Finally have them read the circled 407. Since there is no comma after it, we stop there. So this number is read as "three hundred forty-seven **million**, six hundred twenty-eight **thousand**, four hundred seven."

Place Value					
Whole Numbers					Decimals

hundred trillions / ten trillions / trillions	hundred billions / ten billions / billions	hundred millions / ten millions / millions	hundred thousands / ten thousands / thousands	hundreds / tens / ones	tenths / hundredths / thousandths
Trillions	Billions	Millions	Thousands	Units (ones)	$\frac{1}{10}$ $\frac{1}{100}$ $\frac{1}{1000}$
10^{14} 10^{13} 10^{12}	10^{11} 10^{10} 10^{9}	10^{8} 10^{7} 10^{6}	10^{5} 10^{4} 10^{3}	10^{2} 10^{1} 10^{0}	10^{-1} 10^{-2} 10^{-3}

This approach will help students write multidigit numbers.

Thinking of numbers in groups of three digits will also help students write numbers greater than 999. Using digit lines further simplifies this task. Use the following dialogue to explain the technique:

"Use digits to write 'eighty-two thousand, five hundred three.' "

"How many digits does 'eighty-two' have?" (two)

"Draw two digit lines."   __ __

"Now the word thousand tells you to draw a comma."   __ __,

"Guaranteed, every comma is followed by three digits. Draw three digit lines."   __ __,__ __ __

"Now fill in the digits."   8 2 , 5 0 3

Hint #16:
factors of whole numbers

(Introduce in Lesson 6)

Learning to list the factors in numerical order will help students find the greatest common factor of numbers.

Listing the factors of whole numbers is the first step in finding the greatest common factor (GCF) and will help students reduce fractions by the GCF. Thus, it is very important that students learn to list the factors in numerical order. The procedure is as follows:

1. Always *start* with the number 1.
2. Always *end* with the number given.
3. Then find all the other factors of the given number. (Use "Multiplication Table" on page 3 in the *Adaptations Student Reference Guide*.)
4. List the factors *in order.* Write each factor only *once.* (Example: The factors of 9 are 1, 3, 9.)

Use the following dialogue to explain the technique:

"Let's list all the factors of 12."

"Write the 'start' and 'end' numbers. Leave space to write numbers between."

1   12

"Look down the 2's column in the Multiplication Table, and see if you can find a 12. What number times 2 equals 12?"   (6)

*"Write '2' after the 1. Write '6' **before** the 12."*

1, 2   6, 12

"Look down the 3's column to find a 12. What numbers should we write?"   (3, 4)

1, 2, 3, 4, 6, 12

"The next column we would look down is the 4's. Notice that we have already listed 4 as a factor. This means that we have found all of the factors of 12."

"Look at all the factors. Are they in numerical order?"   (yes)

To review the process described above, ask students to find the factors of 24. (1, 2, 3, 4, 6, 8, 12, 24)

Hint #17:
finding the greatest common factor

(Introduce in Lesson 6)

After students learn to list the factors of numbers, they will then learn to find the common factors of given numbers. It will be a simple step to find the greatest of those common factors. Here is a timesaving shortcut:

1. List (in order) the factors of the smallest number.
2. Instead of listing the factors of the other numbers, look at the factors of the smallest number. **Starting with the greatest factor,** cross out any factor that does not divide evenly into each of the other numbers.
3. Once you find a factor that divides evenly into each of the other numbers, *stop* and circle it. The circled number is the greatest common factor.

Thus, to find the greatest common factor of 8, 20, and 40, first list the factors of 8: 1, 2, 4, 8. Now, starting with the 8, see if these factors divide evenly into both 20 and 40. Eight does not divide evenly into 20, so cross it out. Four divides evenly into 20 and 40, so circle it and stop. Four is the greatest common factor of 8, 20, and 40.

Hint #18:
tests for divisibility
(Introduce in Lesson 6)

Tests for divisibility show whether a number can be divided by 2, 3, 4, 5, 6, 8, 9, or 10.

When checking for the factors of a number, there are a few quick tests for divisibility that will tell the student at a glance if that number can be divided by 2, 3, 4, 5, 6, 8, 9, or 10, without performing the actual division.

When using tests for divisibility, begin with these three questions:

1. Is the last digit 5 or 0? (If so, the number is divisible by 5.)

2. Is the last digit even? (If so, the number is divisible by 2.)

3. What is the sum of the digits? (If the sum is divisible by 3, the number is divisible by 3. If the sum is divisible by 9, the number is divisible by 9.)

Once these three questions have been answered, the other tests for divisibility can be applied more easily.

See the "Tests for Divisibility" chart on page 5 in the *Adaptations Student Reference Guide.*

Tests for Divisibility

A number is able to be divided by . . .

2	if the last digit is even.
4	if the last two digits can be divided by 4.
8	if the last three digits can be divided by 8.
5	if the last digit is 0 or 5.
10	if the last digit is 0.
3	if the **sum of the digits** can be divided by 3.
6	if the number can be divided by 2 **and** by 3.
9	if the **sum of the digits** can be divided by 9.

geometry vocabulary

(Introduce in Lesson 7)

Having students use their arms or fingers to demonstrate the concepts of parallel and perpendicular is usually effective.

Geometric concepts are not difficult, but the vocabulary sometimes is. Some suggestions for teaching various terminology are described below.

- **Parallel/Perpendicular:** One trick is to point out the parallel l's in the word *parallel* to distinguish it from *perpendicular*. Another is to use an example of railroad tracks to describe the concepts. The best method, however, is to have students use their arms or fingers to demonstrate parallel and perpendicular. Be careful that parallel is not always vertical; this may result in confusion when horizontal and oblique parallel lines are introduced.

- **Intersect:** Use the example of a street intersection. Have students show you how their arms can intersect or be parallel. The students should name the words as they demonstrate them.

- **Right angle:** Tell students that the corner of a rectangular piece of paper will fit "just right" into a right angle. Given a variety of obtuse, acute, and right angles, have students hold each one up to the corner of a piece of paper and tell you whether the angle is too small, too big, or "just right." Gradually, the term "right angle" will assume more meaning for the students.

See "Types of Lines" on page 17 and "Types of Angles" on page 18 in the *Adaptations Student Reference Guide*.

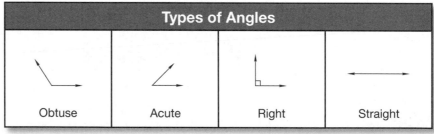

Types of Angles			
Obtuse	Acute	Right	Straight

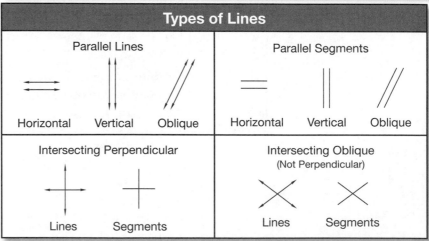

Types of Lines

Parallel Lines			Parallel Segments		
Horizontal	Vertical	Oblique	Horizontal	Vertical	Oblique

Intersecting Perpendicular		Intersecting Oblique (Not Perpendicular)	
Lines	Segments	Lines	Segments

Hint #20:
naming fractions/ identifying fractional parts

(Introduce in Lesson 8)

To help instill the concept of fractional parts, recite "___ out of ___ parts" while pointing to a variety of shaded figures.

The main difficulty students have with identifying fractional parts is that they forget the denominator represents the total possible parts. Thus, many students tend to identify the figure below as one third (naming only the unshaded parts). One solution is to have students recite "___ out of ___ parts" while pointing to the figure. So, for the figure below, have students point to the figure while saying "This shows **one** out of **four** parts."

1 out of 4 parts

Repeated practice with the phrase "___ out of ___ parts" should help. Also, remind students that in fractions the **numerator** (top number) is simply the number of shaded parts. The **denominator** (bottom number) is the total number of parts both shaded and unshaded.

1 out of 3 parts → $\frac{1}{3}$ 5 out of 9 parts → $\frac{5}{9}$

Hint #21:
fraction manipulatives

(Introduce in Lesson 8)

The concept of fractions can be difficult for students who have not moved into the realm of abstract thinking. For these students, it is often helpful to use manipulatives.

Students can make their own pie chart manipulatives using Activity Masters 4–9, which are found in *Saxon Math Course 2 Instructional Masters.* These manipulatives will help students compare fraction parts to see which are larger or smaller.

Students may have difficulty distinguishing between the $\frac{1}{5}$ and $\frac{1}{6}$ sections in the pie charts. Using fraction tower manipulatives may make the differences in fractions easier to see. These are available in the *Adaptations Manipulative Kit.* If you do not have the *Adaptations Manipulative Kit,* instructions for making paper fraction tower manipulatives are given below.

Fractional, Decimal, and Percent Tower™ cubes are available in the Adaptations Manipulative Kit.

Gather scissors, a ruler, and construction paper in a variety of colors. Cut nine strips of construction paper approximately 12 by 2 cm each. Each strip should be the same size but a different color. Using a ruler and scissors, cut eight strips into the following parts: halves, thirds, fourths, fifths, sixths, eighths, tenths, and twelfths. Leave one of the strips whole. When finished, the "whole" strip might be red; the two "$\frac{1}{2}$" strips might be pink; the three "$\frac{1}{3}$" strips might be orange; the four "$\frac{1}{4}$" strips might be yellow; the five "$\frac{1}{5}$" strips might be green; the six "$\frac{1}{6}$" strips might be light blue; the eight "$\frac{1}{8}$" strips might be navy blue; the ten "$\frac{1}{10}$" strips might be purple; and the twelve "$\frac{1}{12}$" strips might be black. After cutting the strips, make sure the "parts" equal the "whole"! Label each part with its correct fraction.

Next, make matching sets of decimal and percent strips. Use the same colors chosen for the fraction set. Thus, if the "$\frac{1}{2}$" fraction strips were pink, make the "0.5" decimal strips and the "50%" percent strips pink also. For example:

When you are finished, can use the strips to compare fractions (such as $\frac{1}{4}$ and $\frac{2}{5}$), to compare percents (10% and 20%), and to compare decimals (0.25 and 0.75). They can also use the strips to compare equivalencies ($\frac{1}{4}$, 0.25, and 25%). Whatever the comparison, the color coding serves as a powerful visual memory tool.

Hint #22:
percent
(Introduce in Lesson 8)

Manipulatives help students grasp the essential relationship between fractions and percents. Students may use the tower manipulative described in Hint #21. Since the towers are color-coded and proportionally sized, students can make a tactile comparison of the two types of towers. For instance, examine the 50% tower and the $\frac{1}{2}$ tower. (Both are the same size and color—pink.) Then compare the 25% tower and the $\frac{1}{4}$ tower (again, same size and color—yellow).

Once students have explored the relationship between fractions and percents using manipulatives, continue to explore more abstract representations such as those provided on page 13 (the "Fraction-Decimal-Percent Equivalents" chart) in the *Adaptations Student Reference Guide.* This chart will help students immensely in subsequent lessons.

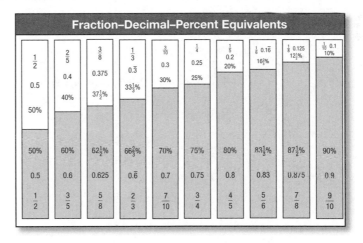

Hint #23:
reading inch rulers
(Introduce in Lesson 8)

The Manipulative Kit contains rulers that can be used with the overhead.

Reading inch rulers is an important life skill for students to learn. But students must first grasp the concept of equivalent fractions to be able to read halves, fourths, eighths, and sixteenths of an inch.

Make a set of transparent rulers using clear plastic sheets. Each ruler should show different fractional divisions. The rulers may be placed on top of each other to demonstrate equivalencies. (One half is really two fourths, etc.) Show students how to count fourths on a quarter-inch ruler (e.g., $\frac{1}{4}$, $\frac{1}{2}$, $\frac{3}{4}$, 1, $1\frac{1}{4}$). This will take much practice before it becomes routine but is worth spending time on because reading rulers is essential in life.

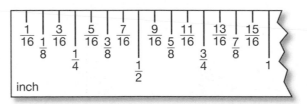

Hint #24:
reciprocal
(Introduce in Lesson 9)

*Use the translation word **flip**, which most students understand to mean "turn upside down."*

Students hear a word such as *reciprocal*, yet may not grasp its meaning. To help students learn new terms, introduce the concept in words that are already in the student's vocabulary.

For the word *reciprocal*, use the translation word *flip*, which most students understand to mean "turn upside down." This provides a mnemonic device for the student to link the new word to. Using the symbol can also be a great help to visual learners.

See "Fraction Terms" on page 12 in the *Adaptations Student Reference Guide.*

Hint #25:
improper fractions
(Introduce in Lesson 10)

Use the cue " 'top heavy' fractions" when referring to improper fractions.

Many students with math difficulties do not comprehend the equivalencies of mixed numbers and improper fractions. First, because the vocabulary can be confusing, try including the description "top heavy" when referring to improper fractions. Fraction tower manipulatives will help demonstrate that is the same amount as $1\frac{1}{4}$. Students will need much tactile practice with this.

Next, demonstrate the concept with two-dimensional pictures such as those shown below. When drawing the figures showing the improper fraction, divide each figure into the same number of parts as the denominator.

Whole number and a fractions $3\frac{2}{3}$ = Improper ("top heavy") fraction $\frac{11}{3}$

Finally, teach the pencil-and-paper approach.

To convert a mixed number to an improper fraction, multiply the denominator by the whole number; then add the numerator. Write this answer over the original denominator.

$$3\frac{2}{3} \longrightarrow 3\frac{2}{3} = \frac{(3 \times 3) + 2}{3} = \frac{11}{3}$$

To convert an improper fraction to a mixed number, divide the numerator by the denominator. The quotient is the whole number, the remainder is the numerator of the fraction, and the divisor is the denominator of the fraction. (The denominator of the fraction does not change from the improper fraction to the mixed number.)

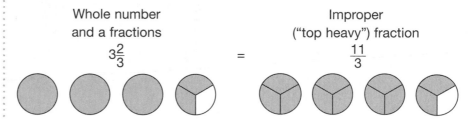

$$\frac{11}{3} \longrightarrow 3\overline{)11}\ ^{3\ R\ 2} \quad \begin{array}{l} \text{numerator} \\ \text{denominator} \end{array} \quad 3\frac{2}{3}$$

Hint #26:
word problem cues
(Introduce in Lesson 11)

Teach students to look for keywords in word problems.

Many students are confused by word problems. Often these students cannot read well and thus do not really understand what is being asked in the question. The textbook identifies word problems as having addition, subtraction, and multiplication patterns.

As an additional help, students should be taught to look for keywords in word problems. Even if they cannot read the rest of a problem, they might see the word *profit* and know to subtract or see the word *average* and know to divide. The chart below shows some common word problem keywords.

Word Problem Keywords			
$+$	$-$	$\times$	$\div$
sum	**difference**	**product**	**quotient**
total, together, joined (after)	profit, before, minus; comparisons such as: more than, less than	times, of, cover, double	each, per, average

Hint #27:
rate
(Introduce in Lesson 13)

By working with the loop method, students will be better prepared to learn about proportion, ratio, and rate.

The following is a simple method that will help students learn about and work with proportion, ratio, rate, and unit pricing. *Although this loop method is not in the* Saxon Math Course 2 *textbook, it is often very helpful to struggling students.*

Students must visualize the problem components and know what to do with them. The procedure is as follows:

1. After reading the word problem, identify the two things the problem is about (miles and hours, money and time, inches and yards, etc.). Write these in a column. (It does not matter which item is placed on top.)

2. Carefully fill in what you know. It is important that the known quantities be written directly across from the items they refer to.

3. Carefully write the information you are looking for, placing a question mark or *X* in the "unknown" spot. Again, make sure that the quantities and question mark are written directly across from the appropriate item names.

4. Draw a loop around the numbers that are diagonally opposite. **The loop should never include the question mark.**

5. Multiply the numbers inside the loop.

- If the number outside the loop is **1**, this "answers" the question mark.

    Example:

    "If you drive your car at 30 miles per hour, how far will you travel in 4 hours?"

    "Name the two things the problem is about."

    mi
    hr

    "Fill in what you know."

    mi $\dfrac{30}{1}$
    hr

    "Fill in what you're looking for."

    mi $\dfrac{30}{1}$ $\dfrac{?}{4}$
    hr

    "Make a diagonal loop and multiply."

         $4 \times 30 = 120$ mi.

    "You'll travel 120 miles in 4 hours."

- If the number outside the loop is **not 1**, divide the "loop" answer by the outside number.

    Example:

    "If Joe reads 2 pages per minute, how long will it take him to read 18 pages?"

    pages $\dfrac{2}{1}$ $\dfrac{18}{?}$ $2\overline{)18}^{\,9}$ minutes
    minutes

    "It will take Joe 9 minutes to read 18 pages."

Students who have solved problems using this loop method will probably adjust easily to the more algebraic format of solving proportions using variables.

See "Proportion (Rate) Problems" on page 19 in the *Adaptations Student Reference Guide* (also shown below).

Proportion (Rate) Problems	
Example 1	Example 2
If the number outside the loop is **1**: $\dfrac{30}{1}\diagdown\dfrac{x}{4}$	If the number outside the loop is **not 1**: $\dfrac{3}{5}\diagdown\dfrac{6}{w}$
Cross multiply. $30 \cdot 4 = x$ $x = 120$	• Cross multiply. $3w = 30$ • Divide by known factor. $30 \div 3 = 10$

Finding missing parts may be better understood by using part-part-whole boxes as a visual representation.

Draw one of the following boxes to represent the two parts and the whole of the problem.

	Percent
Part	
Part	
Whole	100

	Fraction
Part	
Part	
Whole	1

1. First, fill in the whole.

    For percents, the whole is 100%.

    For fractions, the whole is 1.

2. Fill in the part that is known.

3. To find the missing part, subtract the known part from the whole.

Example: Sierra was excited that 87% of her answers were correct. What percent of Sierra's answers were not correct?

1. First, fill in the whole: 100%

2. Fill in the part that is known: 87%

3. To find the missing part, subtract the known part from the whole: $100\% - 87\% = 13\%$

	Percent
Part (correct)	87
Part (not correct)	13
Whole	100

13% of Sierra's answers were not correct.

Example: Solve $p + \dfrac{3}{5} = 1$

1. First, fill in the whole: 1

2. Fill in the part that is known: $\dfrac{3}{5}$

3. To find the missing part, subtract the known part from the whole:

	Fraction
Part (known)	$\dfrac{3}{5}$
Part (unknown)	$\dfrac{2}{5}$
Whole	1

$$p = 1 - \frac{3}{5}$$

$$p = \frac{2}{5}$$

Hint #29:

probability

(Introduce in Lesson 14)

A set of spinners for the overhead is available in the Manipulative Kit.

A strategy for explaining probability follows:

1. Get a spinner with numbers on it. (It does not matter how many numbers.) Ask students to think of some games that use spinners.

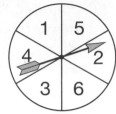

2. Spin the spinner and ask students to name the probability that the spinner will stop on a particular number. Explain that probability means that there are _____ out of _____ possibilities that the spinner will stop on a particular number.

- If it is **certain** to happen, the probability is 1.

   Example:
   "What is the probability that this spinner will stop on a number less than 7?" (1)

- If it is **impossible**, the probability is 0.

   Example:
   "What is the probability that this spinner will stop on the number 8?" (0)

- All other probabilities are stated as fractions (which should be reduced, if possible).

   Example:
   "What is the probability that this spinner will stop on an even number?" ($\frac{3}{6}$, which reduces to $\frac{1}{2}$)

Hint #30:

canceling fractions

(reducing before multiplying)

(Introduce in Lesson 15)

Teaching mental math tricks such as canceling matching zeros or reducing fractions will help students gain confidence in math.

A shortcut that will make multiplication and division of fractions easier is "canceling" (or reducing) fractions before multiplying.

Explain that canceling fractions is simply another term for reducing fractions, a procedure students already know how to do. When fractions are multiplied, any numerator may be paired with any denominator and reduced. Teaching this technique now will not only save students time, but it will also remind them to reduce all fraction answers to their lowest terms.

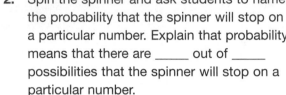

**measuring liquids
and capacities of
containers**

(Introduce in Lesson 16)

There is really no substitute for the use of manipulatives to understand liquid measurements. A set of inexpensive plastic containers (gallon, quart, pint, and cup) can easily be obtained at a discount store; liter bottles are also easy to find. Because working with liquids can be messy, allow students to use pinto beans or other small objects to discover the relationships among various measurements, such as how many cups make a pint.

Once students have a concrete level of understanding of liquid measurements, they will need a "survival tool" to work problems. The chart "Liquids," found on page 1 in the *Adaptations Student Reference Guide* (also shown below), will be useful to students as a tool to work problems.

Have students copy the chart onto notebook paper two or three times. First, write a large G to represent one gallon. Next, write four Q's inside the G to represent the fact that there are four quarts in a gallon. Next, write two P's inside each Q to represent two pints in a quart. Finally, write two c's inside each P to represent two cups in a pint.

*Almost every question
about nonmetric liquid
measurement can be
answered using this chart.*

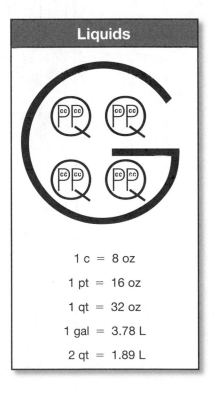

Liquids

1 c = 8 oz

1 pt = 16 oz

1 qt = 32 oz

1 gal = 3.78 L

2 qt = 1.89 L

Almost every question about nonmetric liquid measurement can be answered using this chart. The "Equivalence Table for Units" (shown on page 1 in the *Adaptations Student Reference Guide*) is also useful, but not nearly as memorable as the large "G."

Hint #32:

area and perimeter vocabulary

(Introduce in Lesson 19)

The Manipulative Kit contains color tiles and cubes to help foster a tactile understanding of area, perimeter, and volume.

The problem of distinguishing between the terms *area* and *perimeter* is often one not of concept but of receptive language. One way to help is to give each student a 4" × 6" index card that will represent a backyard. Each student should draw a "fence" around the yard, using the word *perimeter* repeatedly (see example below). With a green crayon, fill in the "grass" with the word *area*. By using both tactile and visual modalities, students will have a better chance to internalize the concepts and vocabulary. (For students who have difficulty writing, print out multiple copies of the words and have the students cut and paste the words onto the cards.) Students should keep their cards in their *Adaptations Student Reference Guides*.

```
PERIMETER PERIMETER PERIMETER
P  AREA AREA AREA AREA AREA AREA AREA  P
E  AREA AREA AREA AREA AREA AREA AREA  E
R  AREA AREA AREA AREA AREA AREA AREA  R
I  AREA AREA AREA AREA AREA AREA AREA  I
M  AREA AREA AREA AREA AREA AREA AREA  M
E  AREA AREA AREA AREA AREA AREA AREA  E
T  AREA AREA AREA AREA AREA AREA AREA  T
E  AREA AREA AREA AREA AREA AREA AREA  E
R  PERIMETER PERIMETER PERIMETER       R
```

See also "Perimeter, Area, Volume" on page 16 in the *Adaptations Student Reference Guide* (also reproduced below).

Perimeter, Area, Volume

Perimeter is the distance around a figure. (Fence)
Label *units.*

$$P \rightarrow \text{add all sides}$$

Area is the enclosed surface of the figure. (Lawn)
Label *square units.* Keyword is "cover."

$$A = l \times w$$

Volume is the amount of space a figure occupies.
Label *cubic units.*

$$V = l \times w \times h$$

*This visual and kinesthetic
exercise will make finding
the perimeter of complex
shapes more tangible for
students.*

To make the abstract exercise of finding the perimeter of complex shapes more tangible for students, it should be both a visual and kinesthetic exercise.

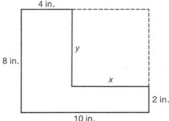

1. Distribute copies of paper with the above shape on it.

2. Hand out two different colors of marking pens.

3. Have each student trace over the **horizontal** sides in one color and the **vertical** sides in another color to reinforce the difference between the two.

4. Point out that although two horizontal sides are labeled with length in inches, one is not. Notice that the horizontal side with unknown length is labeled *x* and the vertical side with unknown length is labeled *y*.

5. To find the length of side *x*, teach students to think through the problem as follows:

> The longest horizontal side is 10 inches.
> Part of that side is 4 inches.
> So side *x* must be 6 inches.
> Label side *x* "6 in."

6. Repeat this process with the vertical sides:

> The longest vertical side is 8 inches.
> Part of that side is 2 inches.
> So side *y* must be 6 inches.
> Label side *y* "6 in."

Once the "unknown" sides have been labeled, finding the perimeter is just a matter of adding.

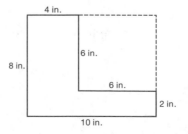

Perimeter = 8 + 4 + 6 + 6 + 2 + 10 = 36 in.

Hint #34:
square roots
(Introduce in Lesson 20)

Use the Multiplication Table in the Adaptations Student Reference Guide to help students learn square roots.

In Lesson 20 students are taught how to find the length of a side of a square when the area is known by finding the square root of the area. A shortcut that can be taught uses the "Multiplication Table" on page 3 in the *Adaptations Student Reference Guide*. Scan the shaded, circled numbers to find the given perfect square (for example, 100). Then look to the top of the circled number's column to find the square root (in this case, 10). This will help students find square roots easily and quickly.

Hint #35:
prime factorization using the factor tree
(Introduce in Lesson 21)

Instruct students to list all prime factors as many times as they are used to form the number.

The textbook offers two methods for prime factorization: the factor tree and division by primes. The first method is far more visual and will likely be easier for the student with special needs. However, at this level it is important that students also learn division by primes. These two methods can be used interchangeably.

When factors of whole numbers were discussed in Lesson 6 and in Hint #16: Factors of Whole Numbers, students were instructed to "list a factor **once.**"

> **Example:** The factors of 9 are 1, 3, and 9.

Now when teaching prime factorization of numbers, instruct students to list **all** prime factors as many times as they are used to form the number.

> **Example:** The *prime* factors of 9 are 3 and 3.

Teach students to circle prime numbers after they write them when completing the factor tree. This makes the process more visual and therefore more memorable. Also, remind students to list the prime numbers in numerical order. This will simplify corrections.

For factor tree problems:

1. List two factors of the given number. If students have difficulty thinking of two factors, prompt them to start with 2, 3, or 5. Even though this may make the factor tree appear lopsided, it helps students get started.
2. Continue to factor until each factor is a prime number.
3. Write the prime factors in order.

Example: Use a factor tree to find the prime factors of 60.

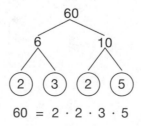

$$60 = 2 \cdot 2 \cdot 3 \cdot 5$$

© 2007 Harcourt Achieve Inc.

Hint #36:
prime factorization using division by primes
(Introduce in Lesson 21)

Teach students to try dividing by the prime numbers 2, 3, or 5 first.

To factor a number using division by primes, write the number in a division box, and begin dividing by the smallest prime number that is a factor. Teach students to try dividing by the prime numbers 2, 3, or 5 first. Continue dividing until the quotient is 1. The divisors are the prime factors of the number.

Example: Factor 420 into prime factors using division by primes.

$$
\begin{array}{r}
2\overline{)420}
\end{array}
\qquad
\begin{array}{r}
105 \\
2\overline{)210} \\
2\overline{)420}
\end{array}
\qquad
\begin{array}{r}
35 \\
3\overline{)105} \\
2\overline{)210} \\
2\overline{)420}
\end{array}
\qquad
\begin{array}{r}
7 \\
5\overline{)35} \\
3\overline{)105} \\
2\overline{)210} \\
2\overline{)420}
\end{array}
\qquad
\begin{array}{r}
1 \\
7\overline{)7} \\
5\overline{)35} \\
3\overline{)210} \\
2\overline{)210} \\
2\overline{)420}
\end{array}
$$

The divisors are the prime factors.
$$420 = 2 \cdot 2 \cdot 3 \cdot 5 \cdot 7$$

Hint #37:
prime factorization of powers of ten
(Introduce in Lesson 21)

Teach students to factor 10 into prime factors and then count the number of zeros in the given number.

To help students factor numbers that are powers of 10, teach them to begin by factoring 10 into prime factors, then to count the number of zeros in the given number.

$10 = 2^1 \cdot 5^1$	10 has one zero, so the exponents of 2 and 5 are 1.
$100 = 2^2 \cdot 5^2$	100 has two zeros, so the exponents of 2 and 5 are 2.
$1000 = 2^3 \cdot 5^3$	1000 has three zeros, so the exponents of 2 and 5 are 3.
$10,000 = 2^4 \cdot 5^4$	10,000 has four zeros, so the exponents of 2 and 5 are 4.
$100,000 = 2^5 \cdot 5^5$	100,000 has five zeros, so the exponents of 2 and 5 are 5.

To help students factor a *large* number that is the product of a number and a power of 10, teach them to expand on the above pattern using the following dialogue and example:

"Write the prime factorization of 4,000,000,000."

"First write 4,000,000,000 as a product of a number and a power of 10."   (4 · 1,000,000,000)

"Write 4 as a product of prime factors."   (2 · 2)

"To find the prime factorization of 1,000,000,000, first count the number of zeros in 1,000,000,000."   (9)

"Remember that the prime factors of 10 are 2 and 5. So the exponents of 2 and 5 for the number 1,000,000,000 are 9." $(1,000,000,000 = 2^9 \cdot 5^9)$

"Now combine the factors." $(2 \cdot 2 \cdot 2^9 \cdot 5^9 = 2^{11} \cdot 5^9)$

Hint #38:
finding square roots using prime factorization
(Introduce in Lesson 21)

To find the square root of a large number, take half of the exponent of each prime factor and multiply.

To help students find the square root of a large number, teach them to use prime factorization.

"Find the square root of 3600."

"Begin by writing the prime factorization of 3600."
($3600 = 2 \cdot 2 \cdot 2 \cdot 2 \cdot 3 \cdot 3 \cdot 5 \cdot 5$)

"Next, write the prime factorization using exponents."
($2^4 \cdot 3^2 \cdot 5^2$)

"Divide each exponent in half."   ($2^2 \cdot 3^1 \cdot 5^1$)

"Now multiply the remaining prime factors to find the square root."   ($2 \cdot 2 \cdot 3 \cdot 5 = 60$)

"The square root of 3600 is 60."

A quick way to sum up this hint:

Take half of the exponent of each prime factor. Multiply.

See "Using Prime Factorization to Find Square Roots" on page 24 in the *Adaptations Student Reference Guide.*

Hint #39:
fraction of a group
(Introduce in Lesson 22)

In problems about a fraction of a group, the whole number is divided by the number of parts indicated by the denominator. For example, $\frac{1}{4}$ of 12 really means to divide 12 into four parts and consider one of those parts. This can be easily demonstrated using plastic tokens or chips; the demonstration will be necessary for students who are at the concrete level of understanding fractions. Students who are at a more abstract level of understanding can use the method described in the textbook.

A cue for this strategy is "Divide by the denominator."

The following "survival strategy" can be used both by students who cannot grasp the concept of fractions and by students who are ready to move beyond drawing pictures of fractions:

- $\frac{1}{2}$ of a number   ⟶   divide by 2

- $\frac{1}{3}$ of a number   ⟶   divide by 3

- $\frac{1}{4}$ of a number   ⟶   divide by 4

A cue for this strategy is "Divide by the denominator."

Often, the numerator will not be 1 in problems about a fraction of a group. Plastic tokens or chips may still be used to provide a tactile demonstration of the concept.

Example: show that $\frac{2}{3}$ of 12 is 8 like this:

XXXX XXXX XXXX

12 is divided into 3 groups.
2 of these 3 groups contain a total of 8.

Another method (more useful with larger numbers) is to have students draw boxes as in the following example:

"Debbie scored two-thirds of the 36 points in the game. How many points did she score?"

36 points

$\frac{2}{3}$ Debbie scored

12 points
12 points

$\frac{1}{3}$ Debbie did not score.

12 points

"Debbie scored 2 x 12 points, which is 24 points."

Another way to solve this problem is to use the loop method previously learned in Hint #27: Rate.

Set up the problem using an "is over of" format:

$$\text{is} \quad \underline{\quad} \quad \underline{\quad}$$
$$\text{of}$$

The question can be reworded, "What **is** $\frac{2}{3}$ **of** 36?" Fill in the known numbers, using a question mark for the unknown number. Then draw a loop around the numbers that are diagonally opposite. The loop should never include the question mark.

is   2   ?
of   3   36

Finally, multiply the two numbers inside the loop ($2 \times 36 = 72$), and divide by the number outside the loop ($72 \div 3 = 24$). Debbie scored 24 points.

See "Finding a Part (Fraction or Percent) When the Whole is Known" on page 14 in the *Adaptations Student Reference Guide*.

Finding a Part (Fraction or Percent) When the Whole is Known
(Alternate Method)

Set up an "is/of" proportion:

• $\frac{2}{3}$ of 600 is what number?

is   2   ?
of   3   600

$(600 \cdot 2) \div 3 = \mathbf{400}$

• 30% of 20 is what number?

$\frac{30}{100} = \frac{3}{10}$ is   3   ?
                       of   10   20

$(20 \cdot 3) \div 10 = \mathbf{6}$

Shortcut: Reduce the ratio before multiplying the numbers in the loop.

To avoid confusion between "LCM" and "GCF," point out that multiple reminds you of multiplication.

Students often confuse the concepts of LCM and GCF. It may be that vocabulary, rather than the mathematical concept, is the problem. Point out that *multiple* reminds you of multiplication, so use the Multiplication Table on page 3 in the *Adaptations Student Reference Guide* to help find the least common multiple. Teach the procedure as follows:

- To find the LCM of 3 and 4, use the table and go down the 3's and 4's columns using your fingers.
- Stop at the first number that 3 and 4 have in common. (12)

Use your index fingers to make a downward motion as you explain the procedure. This visual cue will act as a nonverbal reminder to students. The next time a student asks what the LCM is, use the hand gesture (without saying a word). Students will soon be able to find the LCM independently.

To find the LCM of *larger numbers,* use prime factorization.

See "Using Prime Factorization to Find the LCM " on page 24 in the *Adaptations Student Reference Guide* (and below).

Using Prime Factorization to Find LCM

To find the LCM of larger numbers, such as 18 and 24:

1. Line up the prime factors so that matching digits are above and below each other.
2. Put a line through matching digits. (This cancels one matching digit.)
3. Write the remaining digits in a row and multiply.

$$18: \quad 2 \cdot 3 \cdot 3$$
$$24: \quad 2 \cdot 2 \cdot 2 \cdot 3$$
$$2 \cdot 2 \cdot 2 \cdot 3 \cdot 3 = 72$$

To compute average, add the numbers and divide by the number of items.

The concept of average is not too difficult to convey. It can be demonstrated effectively with manipulatives. For example, give the students twelve plastic tokens divided unevenly into two (or three) groups. Ask the students to rearrange the tokens in two (or three) equal groups. The number in each equal group is the average.

Another method to use for the textbook problems is more abstract, but still fairly simple. Have the students add the numbers and then divide by the number of items. Tell the students that the answer to any average problem will always be between the smallest number and largest number, and that this is a way to "spot check" answers. An example of the procedure follows:

1. To find the average of 24, 26, and 28, first add the numbers:

$$\begin{array}{r} 1 \\ 24 \\ 26 \\ + 28 \\ \hline 78 \end{array}$$

2. Next, divide the sum (78) by the number of items (3):

$$\begin{array}{r} 26 \\ 3\overline{)7^18} \end{array}$$

3. Check the answer (26). The answer must be between the smallest number (24) and the largest number (28).

© 2007 Harcourt Achieve Inc.

Hint #42:
estimating or rounding
(Introduce in Lesson 29)

This procedure for rounding numbers and decimals will work in any situation.

Estimating amounts is one of the most valuable, lifelong skills students can learn. At school, students can use this skill to estimate whether their answers are correct. In other situations, students can estimate how much purchases will cost and whether they have enough money to make those purchases. Most of the time, students will not have number lines available to help them round numbers. The method described below will work in any situation. It shows how to round whole numbers and decimals to any place value.

1. Underline the place value that you will be rounding to (e.g., hundreds place).

2. Circle the digit to its right. (The circle reminds students that this digit will become a zero.)

3. Ask: "Is the circled number 5 or more?"
   If so, add 1 to the underlined number.
   If not, the underlined number stays the same.

4. Replace the circled number (and any numbers after it) with zero.

   Example: Round 5547 to the nearest hundred.

   $$5 \; \underline{5} \; ④ \; 7 \quad \longrightarrow \quad 5 \; 5 \; 0 \; 0$$

Hint #43:
comparing fractions
(Introduce in Lesson 30)

Use this strategy for comparing fractions when manipulatives are not available.

Students will find the following strategy for comparing fractions particularly useful when fraction manipulatives are not available.

Example: Compare: $\quad \frac{1}{2} \; \bigcirc \; \frac{1}{3}$

Cross multiply: $\quad 3 \diagdown \frac{1}{2} \bigcirc \frac{1}{3} \diagup 2$

Then compare the numbers on top:

$3 > 2$, so $\frac{1}{2} \; \bigcirc\!\!>\; \frac{1}{3}$

This is not a difficult concept, but it is easier to learn with a little bit of verbal drill.

1. First, coach students on the vocabulary:

   origin: point where the number lines cross

   x-axis: horizontal number line (*first* number given)

   (Helpful hint to students: Remember, *x* comes before *y* in both the alphabet and rectangular coordinates.)

   y-axis: vertical number line (*second* number given)

2. Next, identify the direction moved from the origin as positive or negative.

   Play a game of "Find Me." On a piece of graph paper (see Activity Master 13 in the *Saxon Math Course 2 Instructional Masters*), label each of the four quadrants with Roman numerals.[†] Say, *"From the origin, I am going negative, then positive. Where am I?"* Have the students say which quadrant you are in. Repeat this type of questioning until you are sure the students can follow directions from the origin, first moving on the *x*-axis, then moving on the *y*-axis.

Play hide-and-seek using rectangular coordinates.

3. If time allows, have the students play hide-and-seek in pairs using rectangular coordinates. Each student has a coordinate plane drawn on paper and marks a hiding place. Then each student takes a turn trying to hit the hiding place of the other student by guessing four different sets of rectangular coordinates. Both students mark the guesses on the coordinate plane. The first one to hit the hiding place of the other wins the game.

See "Rectangular Coordinates" on page 18 in the *Adaptations Student Reference Guide.*

[†]Coordinate plane quadrants are referred to as the first, second, third, and fourth quadrants and are often labeled with Roman numerals (I, II, III, and IV) in a counterclockwise direction beginning with the upper-right quadrant.

coordinate geometry

(Introduce in Investigation 3)

Make multiple copies of the coordinate plane activity worksheets (Activity Master 13 in *Saxon Math Course 2 Instructional Masters*). Store these in a convenient, accessible location. When students need a coordinate plane, instruct them to get a coordinate plane activity worksheet and use it to work the problem.

Hint #46:

decimal place value (digit lines)

(Introduce in Lesson 31)

This approach will help students write decimal numbers.

Students often have difficulty writing the correct digits for written decimal numbers. A simple routine using digit lines will make this task easier. Use the following dialogue to explain the technique:

"Use digits to write 'one hundred twenty-three and one hundred twenty-three thousandths.' "

"How many digits does 'one hundred twenty-three' have?" (three)

"Draw three digit lines."

— — —

"Now the word and *tells you to draw a decimal point."*

— — —.

"The word thousandths *tells you to draw three digit lines after the decimal point."*

— — —.— — —

"Now fill in the digits."

<u>1</u> <u>2</u> <u>3</u> . <u>1</u> <u>2</u> <u>3</u>

The simplicity of this system is that it associates words with decimal points and digit lines. Students can use it to handle decimal numbers of any length.

Decimal Place Values

1,000,000		100,000	10,000	1000		100	10	1	.	$\frac{1}{10}$	$\frac{1}{100}$	$\frac{1}{1000}$	$\frac{1}{10,000}$	$\frac{1}{100,000}$	$\frac{1}{1,000,000}$
millions	,	hundred thousands	ten thousands	thousands	,	hundreds	tens	ones	decimal point	tenths	hundredths	thousandths	ten-thousandths	hundred-thousandths	millionths

Hint #47:
writing numbers
(Introduce in Lesson 31)

A "Spelling Numbers" chart is on page 9 in the Adaptations Student Reference Guide.

Writing numbers correctly will be an important skill for students in later life. One example of using this skill is writing checks. Teach students the following guidelines for writing money amounts on checks:

- Use hyphens in all numbers between 21 and 99 (except those numbers that end with zero).

- Use a comma after the word *thousand* (or any word greater than one thousand that names place value).

- Use the word *and* only at the end of a whole number to indicate that a fraction or decimal will follow. For example, for $201.13, write "two hundred one **and** $\frac{13}{100}$ dollars."

- Use the *ths* ending when writing decimal numbers.

Students may refer to the "Spelling Numbers" chart on page 9 in the *Adaptations Student Reference Guide* to help spell numbers correctly.

Spelling Numbers			
Whole Numbers		**Fractions**	
11	eleven		
12	twelve	$\frac{1}{2}$	one half
13	thirteen		
14	fourteen	$\frac{2}{3}$	two thi<u>rds</u>
15	fifteen	$\frac{3}{5}$	three fi<u>fths</u>
21	twenty-one		
32	thirty-two	$\frac{94}{100}$	ninety-four hundred<u>ths</u>
43	forty-three	$\frac{49}{1000}$	forty-nine thousand<u>ths</u>
54	fifty-four		
65	sixty-five		**Decimals**
76	seventy-six		
87	eighty-seven	0.1	one ten<u>th</u>
98	ninety-eight	0.94	ninety-four hundred<u>ths</u>
123	one hundred twenty-three	0.049	forty-nine thousand<u>ths</u>
1234	one thousand, two hundred thirty-four		

Students often find the most difficult number words to spell are *forty, ninety, nine*, and *four*.

Hint #48:
tenths and hundredths
(Introduce in Lesson 31)

Understanding the difference in value between a tenth and a hundredth is very difficult in the abstract. Try using color tiles for a tactile approach.

Arrange the color tiles in a 10-by-10 array and point out that the large square you formed is made up of 100 parts (10-by-10). Then show one square that represents one of those hundredths. Finally, show one row that demonstrates one tenth (10-by-1). Now ask the students, "If this were solid gold, would you rather have one tenth or one hundredth?" This visual demonstration will make a lasting impression; a simple verbal reminder in future lessons will recall the comparison effectively.

Hint #49:
reading metric rulers
(Introduce in Lesson 32)

Metric rulers that can be used with the overhead are available in the Manipulative Kit.

Many students have had little or no experience measuring objects; thus, it is important to have metric rulers available in the classroom. Teach students to place the zero mark of the ruler even with the end of the item they are measuring. (This will *not* be obvious to many students!) Then ask them to measure anything nearby—their thumbs, their textbooks, their desks, etc.

Students need a clear idea of the length of a centimeter. Try to help them visualize the length of a centimeter compared to an inch.

Next, point to one centimeter on the ruler. Explain that there are ten tiny millimeters in that centimeter. Ask the students how many millimeters are in two centimeters, then five centimeters, then nine centimeters, etc. Ask the students what factor they are multiplying by. (10)

Now point to the seven-centimeter mark and ask how many centimeters are in seventy millimeters. Continue asking questions such as "How many centimeters are in forty millimeters?" or "How many centimeters are in twenty millimeters?" Ask the students what factor they are dividing by. (10) Tell them they have just learned to speak metric!

*Use common classroom
items to compare one
gram to one kilogram.*

Teaching metric weights is much easier with manipulatives. Although students in the United States usually have some sense of how much a pound is, they usually have no such sense of how much a kilogram is. Manipulatives will help.

One suggested activity is to use common classroom items to compare a one-gram mass weight (such as a paper clip) to a one-kilogram mass weight (such as a 2.2-pound book). Explain that the kilogram weighs 1000 times the gram. Ask students if they can think of any other items that weigh about a kilogram.

Also point out the list of metric conversions in the "Equivalence Table for Units" on page 1 in the *Adaptations Student Reference Guide* (also shown below). Although the table helps, the activity is more likely to remain in students' memories.

Equivalence Table for Units

Length

U.S. Customary	Metric
12 in. = 1 ft	10 mm = 1 cm
3 ft = 1 yd	1000 mm = 1 m
5280 ft = 1 mi	100 cm = 1 m
1760 yd = 1 mi	1000 m = 1 km

Weight / Mass

Weight	Mass
U.S. Customary	Metric
16 oz = 1 lb	1000 mg = 1g
2000 lb = 1 ton	1000 g = 1 kg

Capacity (Liquid Measure)

U.S. Customary	Metric
16 oz = 1 pt	1000 mL = 1 L
2 pt = 1 qt	
4 qt = 1 gal	

There are **no common fractions** in the **metric system.** Use **decimals.**

Hint #51:
decimal arithmetic reminders chart
(Introduce in Lesson 35)

The "Decimal Arithmetic Reminders Chart" summarizes the rules for arithmetic with decimal numbers by providing keywords to help students keep track of the decimal point. Across the top of the chart are four operation symbols (+, -, x, ÷). Below each symbol is the rule or memory cue to follow when performing that operation. (There are two kinds of division problems, so there are two different cues.) The chart is on page 7 in the *Adaptations Student Reference Guide*.

Decimal Arithmetic Reminders Chart				
Operation	+ or −	×	÷ by whole (*W*)	÷ by decimal (*D*)
Memory Cue	line up	×; then count	up	over, over, up
	$\pm\overset{\cdot}{\underset{\cdot}{:}}\_\_$	$\times\overset{\cdot}{\underline{\underline{}}}$	$W\overline{)\overset{\cdot}{}}$	$D.\overline{)\overset{\cdot}{}}$

You may need to . . .
• Place a decimal point to the right of a whole number.
• Fill empty places with zeros.

Hint #52:
complex average
(Introduce in Lesson 55)

One basic graphic may help students better comprehend and remember how to solve complex average problems.

When teaching complex average, it is recommended that you use graphics as well as words to help students remember the concepts. The "Complex Average" chart on page 25 in the *Adaptations Student Reference Guide* presents the complex average concepts in words. The following graphic may help students comprehend and remember how to solve complex averages:

$$\text{number of items}\overline{)\overset{\text{average}}{\text{sum}}}$$

If students remember this one basic graphic, they can use it to solve complex average problems in the following ways:

- To find a **missing sum** of an average:
  average × number of items = missing sum
  Remember this:
  $$\text{number of items}\overline{)\overset{\text{average}}{\text{sum}}}$$
  To find a missing dividend (the sum), multiply:
  $$\begin{array}{r}\text{average}\\ \times\ \underline{\text{number of items}}\\ \text{missing sum}\end{array}$$

- To find a **missing number** from an average:
  1. average × number of items = sum
  2. add the known numbers = sum of known numbers
  3. Sum − sum of known numbers = missing number

  Or graphically:
  1.
  $$\text{number of items}\overline{)\overset{\text{average}}{\text{sum}}} \longrightarrow \begin{array}{r}\text{average}\\ \times\ \underline{\text{number of items}}\\ \text{sum}\end{array}$$

  2.
  $$\begin{array}{r}\text{known number}\\ +\ \underline{\text{known number}}\\ \text{sum of known numbers}\end{array}$$

  3.
  $$\begin{array}{r}\text{sum}\\ -\ \underline{\text{sum of known numbers}}\\ \text{missing number}\end{array}$$

Rather than a graphic for the third type of complex average problem, an example is used to illustrate the procedure.

- To find a **missing number** that makes a new average:
  1. average A × number of items = sum A
  2. average B × total number of items = sum B
  3. sum B − sum A = missing number

Example: After 4 tests, Annette's average score was 89. What score does Annette need on her fifth test to bring her average up to 90%?

1. average A × number of items = sum A
   89 × 4 = 356
2. average B × total number of items = sum B
   90 × 5 = 450
3. sum B − sum A = missing number
   450 − 356 = 94

Annette needs a 94 on her fifth test.

Hint #53:
classifying
quadrilaterals

*(Introduce in
Investigation 6)*

*Review the qualities
of each quadrilateral by
asking "Is every …,"
"Are some …"
type questions.*

Questions such as "Is every square a rhombus?" require a high level of abstract thinking. Use the "Quadrilaterals" chart on page 18 in the *Adaptations Student Reference Guide* (also shown below) to help answer the question. Review the qualities of each quadrilateral with students. Point to the chart and ask "Is every …," "Are some …" type questions. Also have students ask those types of questions.

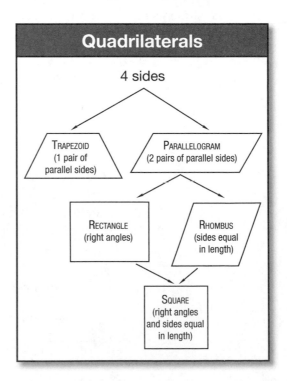

Hint #54:
geometric solids
(manipulatives)
(Introduce in Lesson 67)

The ETA Relational GeoSolids set is available in the Manipulative Kit.

There is really no substitute for manipulatives. Useful ones to have are a cube, a rectangular prism, a square-based pyramid, a triangular-based pyramid, a triangular prism, a sphere, a cone, and a cylinder.

Students will be asked to count the faces, edges, and vertices of these solids. Because many students get lost when counting the number of faces, it helps to paint or put a colored sticker on at least one side of each solid. A better alternative is to buy the ETA Relational GeoSolids set, which is available in the *Adaptations Manipulative Kit*. These clear plastic manipulatives are green on one side, helping students keep track of the number of faces. The set also includes a triangular-based pyramid, which is often difficult to find.

The more tactile experiences students have, the sooner they will be able to move to more abstract mathematical thinking.

Hint #55:
faces on a cube
(Introduce in Lesson 67)

Enhance students' conception of spatiality by making a metric box.

Although it is possible to simply tell students that cubes have six faces, this would require that they memorize yet another fact; it is more effective to enhance their conception of spatiality. One way to do this is to make a cube called a *metric box*. Start with a sheet of paper or thin cardboard that is 30 by 40 cm (about 12 by 16 inches). Divide the sheet into twelve 10-by-10-cm squares. Now cut out the "t" shape and fold as shown.

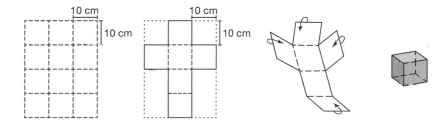

Each edge of the completed cube should be 10 cm long. Each face should be 10 by 10 cm. This cube would hold one liter of water. The weight (mass) of the water in this cube would be one kilogram.

If it is not possible for every student to make a cube, consider laminating and creasing a "master" cube for class use. Students will want to fold and unfold the cube many times as they discover that the t-shaped paper forms a cube.

Hint #56:

surface area
of a prism

(Introduce in Lesson 67)

Cardboard boxes can help students visualize the concept of calculating the surface area of a prism.

To help students visualize the concept of calculating the surface area of a prism, guide them through the following exercise:

1. Get three colors of self-adhesive paper (red, white, and blue) and a rectangular box with a top.

2. Cut the edges of the box so that it is in one piece and lies flat (see graphic below).

3. Cover both side ends with red.

4. Cover the top and bottom with white.

5. Cover the front and back with blue.

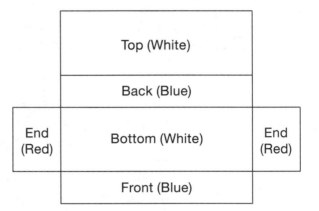

6. Have students calculate the area of each **piece**; point out that this only needs to be done to three of the pieces. There are two identical red pieces, two identical white pieces, and two identical blue pieces.

7. Ask the students if they can find a shortcut to calculate the surface area of the prism.
   (Shortcut: 2 × top + 2 × back + 2 × end = surface area)

8. Keep the covered box for students to refer to in the future.

Hint #57:
volume
(Introduce in Lesson 70)

Colored cubes, available in the Manipulative Kit, are an effective way to teach the concept of volume.

Volume is best taught by using manipulatives. Use the colored cubes in the *Adaptations Manipulative Kit* (or sugar cubes). Once students have mastered the concept using objects, it will be easy to use the formula $V = l \times w \times h$. Show students the formulas for volume on pages 16 and 30 in the *Adaptations Student Reference Guide*.

Example: Find the number of 1-cm cubes that can fit in the box shown.

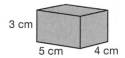

To find the volume of a rectangular prism:

1. Find the number of cubes in one layer of the rectangular prism. (This equals the area of the *base* of the prism.)

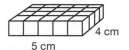

one layer

$5 \times 4 = 20$ cubes

$\begin{array}{cc} \text{layers} & 1 \\ \text{cubes} & \overline{20} \end{array}$

2. Multiply the number of cubes in one layer by the number of layers in the prism (the *height* of the prism.)

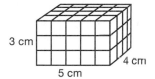

three layers

$\begin{array}{cc} \text{layers} & 1 \quad 3 \\ \text{cubes} & 20 \quad ? \end{array}$

$20 \times 3 = 60$ cubes

Remind students that volume may be expressed different ways (using the answer in the above example):

60 cm^3, 60 cu. cm, or 60 cubic centimeters

In Lesson 39 students were taught that a proportion is a statement of two equal ratios and that missing terms in proportions can be found using cross products. In Lesson 97 students use proportions to find the length of an unknown side of a triangle and to solve indirect measure problems.

Understanding proportion setups can be confusing. Arbitrarily placing numbers in the setups may produce incorrect answers. The following examples demonstrate correct ways proportions can be set up.

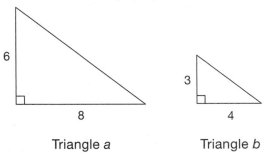

Triangle *a*   Triangle *b*

Proportion Setups	Examples	
	Proportions	Cross Products
A proportion may be written by setting the ratio of one set of corresponding sides equal to another set of corresponding sides from similar triangles.	$\frac{6}{3} = \frac{8}{4}$	$6 \cdot 4 = 3 \cdot 8$ $24 = 24$
	$\frac{4}{8} = \frac{3}{6}$	$4 \cdot 6 = 8 \cdot 3$ $24 = 24$
A proportion may also be written by setting the ratio of two sides of one triangle equal to the ratio of their corresponding sides in a similar triangle.	$\frac{6}{8} = \frac{3}{4}$	$6 \cdot 4 = 3 \cdot 8$ $24 = 24$
	$\frac{4}{3} = \frac{8}{6}$	$4 \cdot 6 = 3 \cdot 8$ $24 = 24$

Notice that all four of the cross products are identical. This shows that all four proportions are equivalent. Therefore, any of these setups can be used to find the length of an unknown side of a triangle.

Emphasize to students that the corresponding sides are always placed directly across (horizontally) or down (vertically) from each other in the proportion setup. For example, notice in Triangles *a* and *b* above that 6 and 3 are corresponding sides and are always placed either horizontally or vertically from each other in the proportion setups. Unrelated sides will always be diagonal from each other in the proportion setup. Again, notice that 8 and 3 are always diagonal from each other since they are completely unrelated—they are *not* corresponding sides, nor are they sides from the same triangle. Remembering this horizontal/vertical guideline will help students set up proportions correctly.

Hint #59:

scale factor

(Introduce in Lesson 98)

Teach students to write and solve an equation using f for the scale factor.

Teach students to "divide the corresponding sides" as a shortcut in calculating the scale factor.

The scale factor is the number of times larger (or smaller) the terms of one ratio are when compared with the terms of the other ratio.

Example: What is the scale factor from $\frac{3}{4}$ to $\frac{18}{24}$?

$$\frac{3}{4} \times \frac{6}{6} = \frac{18}{24}$$

The scale factor is 6 because the terms of the second ratio are 6 times the terms of the first ratio.

One way to find the scale factor is to select any pair of corresponding sides of two similar figures. Write an equation using f for the scale factor and solve for f.

Example: Calculate the scale factor (f) from the smaller triangle to the larger triangle.

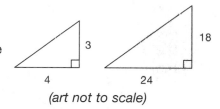

(art not to scale)

(side of figure starting **from**) $\cdot$ f = (side of figure going **to**)

$$3 \cdot f = 18$$
$$f = 6$$

A shortcut to finding the scale factor is to divide the corresponding sides.

The side of the figure going **to** is the numerator (dividend).
The side of the figure starting **from** is the denominator (divisor).

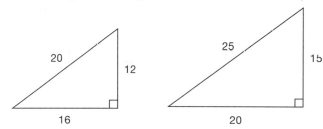

Examples: Calculate the scale factor from the smaller triangle to the larger triangle using the "divide the corresponding sides" shortcut.

To the larger triangle $\longrightarrow$ $\frac{25}{20} = 1.25$
From the smaller triangle $\longrightarrow$

Calculate the scale factor from the larger triangle to the smaller triangle using the "divide the corresponding sides" shortcut.

To the smaller triangle $\longrightarrow$ $\frac{20}{25} = .08$
From the larger triangle $\longrightarrow$

The scale factor can also be used to compare the *area* and *volume* of two similar figures. The scale factor *squared* times the area of the first figure equals the area of the second figure. The area of the smaller triangle above is 96 units^2. Since the scale factor from the smaller to the larger triangle is 1.25, the area of the larger triangle is $(1.25)^2$ (that is, the scale factor squared) times the area of the smaller triangle.

$$(1.25)^2 \times 96 = 1.5625 \times 96 = 150 \text{ units}^2$$

Proof: Area of the larger triangle is one half the base times height:

$$\frac{1}{\underset{1}{2}} \times \overset{10}{\cancel{20}} \times 15 = 150 \text{ units}^2$$

Likewise, when calculating the *volume* of two similar figures, the scale factor *cubed* times the volume of the first figure equals the volume of the second figure.

See "Scale Factor" on page 31 in the *Adaptations Student Reference Guide.*

- *Scale factor* is the number of times larger or smaller the terms of one ratio are when compared with the terms of the other ratio.

- Scale factor will be expressed in decimal form, unless otherwise directed.

- The relationship between the *areas* of two similar figures is the scale factor *squared*.

- The relationship between the *volumes* of two similar figures is the scale factor *cubed*.

Hint #60:
comparing volume
(Introduce in Lesson 113)

ETA Relational GeoSolids are available in the Manipulative Kit.

By the time students reach this lesson, they probably understand the difference between the surface area and volume of a figure. In Lesson 113 students look at volume comparisons.

The following experiment will help students discover the relationship between the volume of a cylinder and the volume of a cone. Using the ETA Relational GeoSolids from the Manipulative Kit, remove the green lids from the large cylinder and the large cone with equal bases and heights. Holding up both containers, ask students to predict whether the containers will hold equal or different amounts. Then fill the cone with water, sand or rice. Empty the contents of the cone into the cylinder. Students will see that the cylinder is about one third full.

Challenge students to predict how many times the cone must be filled in order to fill the cylinder. Continue filling the cone and pouring its contents into the cylinder until the cylinder is full. Discuss the relationship between the volume of a cylinder and cone of equal base and height.

This experiment can also be done with pyramids/cubes and cylinders/spheres. If purchased manipulatives are not available, use everyday items such as a soup can for a cylinder and a cone-shaped paper cup (with the same base measurement).

As students develop their understanding of volume, let them estimate the volume before they actually do any calculating or measuring. Using the manipulatives will give students visual confirmation of the formulas. Once they know the formula for the volume of a cylinder, help them visualize a cone within that cylinder and remind them that the cone only takes up one third of the space.

Charts

Targeted Practices provide additional practice for the more challenging lessons.

This section charts the topics covered by the Targeted Practice, Fraction Activities, and Concept Posters and indicates the ideal lesson for their use.

Although the _Saxon Math Course 2_ textbook contains sufficient practice for most students to learn the concepts, some students might require additional practice to fully grasp certain topics. In a self-paced environment, it is suggested that students work each Targeted Practice. In an inclusion environment, assign them as needed.

Use with Lesson	Targeted Practice Topic
1	Subtracting Across Zeros
1	Multiplying by One- and Two-Digit Numbers
1	Dividing by One- and Two-Digit Numbers
2	Properties of Operations
3	Missing Numbers in Arithmetic Problems
6	Tests for Divisibility
9	Adding and Subtracting Fractions with Like Denominators
10	Mixed Numbers and Improper Fractions
13	Problems About Equal Groups
14	Problems About Parts of a Whole
15	Reducing Fractions
17	Finding Angle Measures with a Protractor
19	Perimeter of Complex Shapes
20	Simplifying Expressions with Exponents
21	Prime Factorization
23	Adding and Subtracting Mixed Numbers with Like Denominators
26	Multiplying and Dividing Fractions and Mixed Numbers
27	Least Common Multiple (LCM)
29	Rounding Fractions and Mixed Numbers
30	Adding and Subtracting Fractions and Mixed Numbers with Unlike Denominators
31	Writing Decimal Numbers
33	Rounding Decimal Numbers
35	Adding and Subtracting Decimal Numbers
37	Area of Complex Shapes
43	Converting Decimals to Fractions and Fractions to Decimals

Use with Lesson	Targeted Practice Topic
45	Dividing by Decimal Numbers
48	Fraction-Decimal-Percent Equivalents
49	Adding and Subtracting Mixed Measures
50	Unit Multipliers
52	Order of Operations and Evaluation
57	Negative Exponents
60	Fraction, Percent, and Decimal Parts of a Number
64	Adding Positive and Negative Numbers
65	Circumference
68	Algebraic Addition
69	Proper Form of Scientific Notation
75	Area of Complex Figures
77	Percent of a Number, Part 2
Inv. 8	Compound Probability
82	Area of Circles
83	Multiplying Numbers in Scientific Notation
84	Collecting Algebraic Terms
85	Order of Operations with Positive and Negative Numbers
87	Multiplying Algebraic Terms
89	Finding Interior and Exterior Angles of Regular Polygons
93	Two-Step Equations
96	Distributive Property with Algebraic Terms
97	Indirect Measure
98	Scale Factor
99	Pythagorean Theorem
100	Estimating Square Roots
101	Translating Expressions into Equations
102	Simplifying Equations
107	Slope of a Line
109	Equations with Exponents
111	Dividing in Scientific Notation
115	Factoring Algebraic Expressions
116	Slope-Intercept Form of Linear Equations

Fraction Activities

Fraction Activities aid the transition from tactile to pencil-and-paper tasks involving fractions.

Fraction Activity worksheets are one-page worksheets designed to be completed with the use of manipulatives. They provide extra practice for students who struggle with fraction concepts.

Fraction Activity	Use with Lesson	Topic
A	8	Fraction-Decimal-Percent Equivalents
B	Inv. 1	Comparing Fractions and Percents
C	11	Comparing Fractions
D	15	Equivalent Fractions
E	16	Reducing Mixed Numbers
F	22	Subtracting from a Whole Number

Concept Posters

Concept Posters may be posted in the classroom as quick, easy references for students. Some may be enlarged and used as posters. Or there may be a need to make individual copies for students to have close at hand.

Use with Lesson	Name of Poster
1	Number Families
7	Angles and Triangles
8	Examples of Spelling Numbers
8	Often Used Fractions
11	Word Problem Keywords
16	Liquids
Inv. 2	Circle
21	Primes and Composites

Individualized Education Plans

See a sample IEP form on page 87.

A list of short-term Individualized Education Plan (IEP) objectives for *Saxon Math Course 2* is provided on pages 84-86. Each objective is followed by the lesson number after which the concept is tested. Since the concept will be practiced as least ten times (on the Adaptations testing schedule) before it is tested, most students achieve 80% accuracy. With this list of IEP objectives, teachers may determine which objectives have already been met and which should be objectives for the coming year.

These short-term instructional objectives are in a ready-to-use format. Teachers may copy and complete a set of the pages for each student or just use the list to select certain objectives for each studen's IEP. Teachers may also input these objectives on a computer, make a copy of the file for each student, and delete the portions that do not apply to a particular student.

Short-Term Instructional Objectives for *Saxon Math Course 2*

Instructional Objectives:	Date Projected:	Evaluation Results:

- Given a series of written computation and word problems involving **fractions,** the student will complete them with 80 percent accuracy as measured by teacher-made tests.

	Date Projected:	Evaluation Results:
1. Reducing and converting by prime factorization (34)	_____	_____
2. Multiplying and dividing mixed numbers (36)	_____	_____
3. Adding and subtracting mixed numbers with different denominators (40)	_____	_____
4. Finding the whole when a fraction is known (81)	_____	_____

- Given a series of written computation and word problems involving **decimals and percents,** the student will complete them with 80 percent accuracy as measured by teacher-made tests.

	Date Projected:	Evaluation Results:
1. Adding, subtracting, and multiplying decimals (45)	_____	_____
2. Dividing decimals by decimals (55)	_____	_____
3. Fraction, decimal, and percent equivalents (58)	_____	_____
4. Finding the percent of a whole (70)	_____	_____
5. Finding the whole when a percent is known (87)	_____	_____
6. Percent of change (102)	_____	_____

- Given a series of written problems involving **number theory,** the student will demonstrate understanding by working them with 80 percent accuracy as measured by teacher-made tests.

	Date Projected:	Evaluation Results:
1. Sequences, patterns, and divisibility rules (16)	_____	_____
2. Prime factorization (31)	_____	_____
3. Estimating whole numbers and decimals by rounding (43)	_____	_____
4. Comparing whole numbers, fractions, and decimals (43)	_____	_____
5. Graphing inequalities (88)	_____	_____

Instructional Objectives (continued):

- Given a series of written computation and word problems involving **money concepts,** the student will complete them with 80 percent accuracy as measured by teacher-made tests.

  1. Rounding money to the nearest dollar (43)
  2. Sales Tax (56)
  3. Commission and profit (70)
  4. Markup and markdown (102)
  5. Simple and compound interest (120)

- Given a series of written problems involving the **interpretation of graphs and tables,** the student will complete them with 80 percent accuracy as measured by teacher-made tests.

  1. Plotting rectangular coordinates (41)
  2. Bar, line, and pie graphs (61)
  3. Graphing functions (101)
  4. Graphing nonlinear equations (120)

- Given a series of written problems involving **geometry,** the student will complete them with 80 percent accuracy as measured by teacher-made tests.

  1. Measuring angles using protractor (27)
  2. Classifying quadrilaterals and triangles (72)
  3. Transformations (90)
  4. Calculating circumference and area of circles (92)
  5. Pythagorean theorem (109)
  6. Angle bisectors (111)
  7. Calculating perimeter and area of complex shapes (114)
  8. Calculating surface area of prisms (115)
  9. Calculating volume of pyramids, cones, and spheres (120)

- Given a series of written computation and word problems involving **measurement,** the student will complete them with 80 percent accuracy as measured by teacher-made tests.

  1. U.S. Customary System of length, liquid, and weight (26)
  2. Metric system of length, liquid, and weight (42)
  3. Adding, subtracting, and converting mixed measures (59)
  4. Unit multipliers and unit conversion (98)
  5. Volume, capacity, and mass (120)

- Given a series of written problems involving **algebraic concepts,** the student will complete them with 80 percent accuracy as measured by teacher-made tests.

  1. Order and comparing integers (14)
  2. Negative exponents (67)
  3. Adding and subtracting signed numbers (78)
  4. Multiplying and dividing signed numbers (83)
  5. Algebraic terms (94)
  6. Negative coefficients (100)
  7. Evaluating expressions with variables and signed numbers (101)
  8. Factoring algebraic expressions (120)

Instructional Objectives (continued):

- Given a series of written problems involving **exponents,** the student will demonstrate understanding by working them with 80 percent accuracy as measured by teacher-made tests.

    1. Evaluating exponential expressions (30)
    2. Square roots of perfect squares (30)
    3. Multiplying by powers of ten (57)
    4. Large and small numbers in scientific notation (67)
    5. Multiplying numbers in scientific notation (93)
    6. Order of operations with signed numbers and exponents (95)
    7. Estimating square roots (110)
    8. Equations with exponents (119)

- Given a series of written computation and word problems involving **ratio and proportion,** the student will complete them with 80 percent accuracy as measured by teacher-made tests.

    1. Simple proportion (49)
    2. Writing rates as ratios (56)
    3. Simple ratio (64)
    4. Implied ratio (82)
    5. Using proportion to solve percent problems (91)
    6. Scale and scale factor (108)

- Given a series of written problems involving **statistics and probability,** the student will complete them with 80 percent accuracy as measured by teacher-made tests.

    1. Mean, median, mode, and range (51)
    2. Average of two or more groups (65)
    3. Simple probability, chance and odds (90)
    4. Compound probability (104)

School District
Special Education Local Plan Area
Instructional Plan—Goals and Objectives

Student's Name **Tanesha Doe**   IEP Date **8/16/06**

❑ RS ❑ SC ❑ Home/Hospital

Annual Goal(s)

Tanesha will improve in calculation and math applications.

Present Level of Performance

She is in the early stages of multiplying fractions.

Instructional Objectives	Date Projected	Evaluation Results
Given a series of written computation and word problems involving **fractions,** the student will complete them with 80 percent accuracy.		
1. Reducing and converting by prime factorization (34)		
2. Multiplying and dividing mixed numbers (36)		
3. Adding and subtracting mixed numbers with different denominators (40)		
4. Finding the whole when a fraction is known (81)		
Given a series of written computation and word problems involving **ratio and proportion,** the student will complete them with 80 percent accuracy.		
1. Simple proportion (49)		
2. Writing rates as ratios (56)		
3. Simple ratio (64)		
4. Implied ratio (82)		
5. Using proportion to solve percent problems (91)		
6. Scale and scale factor (108)		
Given a series of written problems involving **statistics and probability,** the student will complete them with 80 percent accuracy.		
1. Mean, median, mode, and range (51)		
2. Average of two or more groups (65)		
3. Simple probability, chance, and odds (90)		
4. Compound probability (104)		

Method of Evaluation ❑ Observation ❑ Criterion Referenced Tests ❑ Teacher-Made Tests

❑ Standardized Tests ❑ Other_____

Needed Specialized Equipment and Services

Summary of Progress *(To be completed at next IEP meeting)*

Suggested Reading

Armstrong, Thomas. *In Their Own Way: Discovering and Encouraging Your Child's Personal Learning Style*. Los Angeles: J.P. Tarcher, 1998.

Hallahan, Daniel, James Kauffman, and John Wills Lloyd. *Introduction to Learning Disabilities*. Boston: Allyn and Bacon, 1996.

Harwell, Joan M. *Complete Learning Disabilities Handbook: Ready-to-Use Techniques for Teaching Learning-Handicapped Students*. West Nyack, NY: Center for Applied Reasearch in Education, 1989.

Lavoie, Richard. *It's So Much Work to Be Your Friend*. New York: Touchstone, 2005

Osman, Betty B. *Learning Disabilities: A Family Affair*. New York: Warner Books, 1990.

Parker, Harvey C. *The ADD Hyperactivity Handbook for Schools: Effective Strategies for Identifying and Teaching Students with Attention Deficit Disorders in Elementary and Scondary Schools*. Platation, FL: Impact Publications, 1992.

Platt, Jennifer M. and Judy L. Olson. *Teaching Adolescents with Mild Disabilities*. Pacific Grove, CA: Brooks/Cole Publishers, 1996.

Silver, Larry B. *The Misunderstood Child: Understanding and Coping With Your Child's Learning Disabilities*. New York: Times Books, 1998.

Smith, Corinne and Lisa W. Strick. *Learning Disabilities: A to Z. A Parent's Complete Guide to Learning Disabilities from Preschool to Adulthood*. New York: Free Press Publications, 1997.

Smith, Sally L. *No Easy Answers; The Learning Disabled Child at Home and at School*. New York: Bantam Books, 1995.

Stevens, Suzanne H. *The LD Child and ADHD Child: Ways Parents and Professionals Can Help*. Winston-Salem, NC: John F. Blair Publications, 1996.

Wender, Paul H. *The Hyperactive Child, Adolescent, and Adult: Attention Deficit Disorder Through the Lifespan*. New York: Oxford University Press, 1987.

Young, Rosalie and Harriet H. Savage. *How to Help Students Overcome Learning Problems and Learning Disabilities: Better Learning for All Ages*. 2nd ed. Danville, IL: Interstate Printers and Publishers, 1989.

Suggested Viewing

Beyond FAT City: A Look Back, A Look Ahead (2005)
Seventy-minute video with discussion guide. Order online: http://ldonline.learningstore.org/. Order by phone: (800) 542-9714.

How Difficult Can This Be? A Learning Disabilities Workshop (F.A.T. City) (1989)
Seventy-minute video with discussion guide. Order onliine: http://ldonline.learningstore.org/. Oder by phone: (800) 542-9714.

Learning Disabilities and Discipline with Richard Lavoie: When the Chips are Down . . . Strategies for Improving Children's Behavior (1997)
Sixty-two-minute video and discussion guide. Order onliine: http://ldonline.learningstore.org/. Oder by phone: (800) 542-9714.

Learning Disabilities and Social Skills with Richard Lavoie: Last One Picked . . . First One Picked On (1994)
Sixty-eight-minute teacher version video with teacher's guide or sixty-two-minute parent version video with parent's guide. Order onliine: http://ldonline.learningstore.org/. Oder by phone: (800) 542-9714.

Related Organizations

Children and Adults with Attention-Deficit/Hyperactivity Disorder (CHADD)
8181 Professional Place, Suite 201
Landover, MD 20785
(800) 233-4050 or (301) 306-7070
www.chadd.org

The Council for Exceptional Children (CEC)
1110 North Globe Road, Suite 300
Arlington, VA 22201-5704
(888) CEC-SPED or (703) 620-3660
www.cec.sped.org

The International Dyslexia Association (IDA)
(formerly Orton Dyslexia Society)
8600 LaSalle Road
Chester Building, Suite 382
Baltimore, MD 21286-2044
(800) ABCD123 or (410) 296-0232
www.interdys.org

Learning Disablities Association (LDA)
4156 Library Road
Pittsburgh, PA 15234-1349
(412) 341-1515
www.ldanatl.org

National Center for Learning Disablities (NCLD)
381 Park Avenue South, Suite 1401
New York, NY 10016
(888) 575-7373 or (212) 545-7510
222.ncld.org

Teacher Notes